INSIGHT COMPACT GUIDES

Bath

& SURROUNDINGS

Compact Guide: Bath is the ideal quick-reference guide to this world-famous city. It tells you all you need to know about Bath's attractions, from ancient baths to elegant squares and crescents, through fascinating museums and to beautiful waterways and gardens. Also included are excursions into the surrounding area.

This is just one title in *Apa Publications'* new series of pocket-sized, easy-to-use guidebooks intended for the independent-minded traveller. *Compact Guides* pride themselves on being up-to-date and authoritative. They are in essence mini travel encyclopedias, designed to be comprehensive yet portable, as well as readable and reliable.

Star Attractions

An instant reference to some of Bath's most popular tourist attractions to help you on your way.

The Great Bath p19

Royal Crescent p22

Bath Abbey p20

Assembly Rooms p24

Bradford-on-Avon p37

Wells Cathedral p46

Longleat p52

Stonehenge p54

Stourhead p54

BaTH
& SURROUNDINGS

Bath – A Georgian Jewel

Bath makes a striking first impression, especially on anyone approaching the city by car from the heights of Lansdown, Swainswick or Claverton. The stunning configuration of crescents, squares and terraces that unfolds below is a triumphant manifestation of the Augustan Age of Reason. Here order and precision combine with lightness and grace, satisfying both the mind and the senses. But Bath is not only famed for its superb Georgian architecture; at its elegant heart are the Roman baths, the most impressive Roman remains in Britain with the possible exception of Hadrian's Wall.

Location and size

Aerial view of the Upper Town
The Roman Great Bath

The city lies cradled in the soft downs of the Mendip Hills, the source of its famous pale stone as well as the hot springs that have been its *raison d'être* since Celtic times. Dissected by the Avon river, which flows into the Severn estuary at Avonmouth, the Kennet and Avon Canal (1810) and the Great Western Railway (1841), the city covers 11 hilly sq miles (29sq km). It centres on the ancient Abbey and Roman Baths, with Georgian Bath spreading north to the Upper Town and east over the river to Bathwick, and most modern development squeezed into Kingsmead to the south.

5

The city has 84,000 inhabitants, though this number is swelled by some 2 million tourists a year, not to mention out-of-towners who come for its excellent shops, restaurants, theatre and concerts. While in many minds the city is associated with genteel, middle-class retirees (after all, the Bath chair was invented here), in actual fact its population is an invigorating mix of young and old, a large number of the former at Bath University, established on Claverton Down in 1966, and the City of Bath College in the centre.

Music man

The city is also a magnet for artists, musicians and craftspeople, and in recent years several prominent members of the British media have made it their main home instead of London (ensuring increased news coverage of the controversial Batheaston and Swainswick bypass which has been carved through the Avon Valley despite feisty opposition from many Bath residents). With no home at all are a disproportionately large number of 'crusties' and other vagrants whose begging prompts sporadic protest as far away as Westminster. There is nothing very new in this. In the 16th century two acts of Parliament concerning vagrancy specifically mentioned Bath.

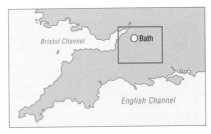

UNESCO symbol outside the Pump Room

A stylish busker
Gorgon head, the Roman Baths

World Heritage Site

In 1988 Bath was designated a World Heritage Site by UNESCO, uniquely for a complete British city. This means it is considered a site of outstanding historical importance whose 'loss, through deterioration or disappearance...constitutes an impoverishment of the heritage of all the peoples of the world'. As such it is eligible for grants from the World Hertiage Fund to help preserve its buildings.

On a local level, key defenders of the city's heritage are Bath City Council's Conservation Committee and the Bath Preservation Trust, a long-established body which monitors the council's work and keeps it on its toes. The trust's work ranges from major restorations of historic buildings (of which there are almost 5,000), such as Beckford's Tower on Lansdown Hill, to ensuring even the smallest repair to a listed structure – from a drain grille to a bell pull – is as far as possible in keeping with the Georgian original. This has led to some well-publicised battles between the Trust and local residents, including one centring on a yellow door (instead of the prescribed white or stripped wood) right in the middle of the Royal Cresent. Arbitration was eventually referred to the highest court in the land, the House of Lords, resulting in victory for the resident. However, the degree of opposition was heeded and the shade of yellow was toned down from vibrant buttercup to pale primrose.

There is also a conflict of interests between excavating the archaeological remains and preserving the city's fine Georgian heritage. The Roman baths we see today are just a small portion of the total Roman complex, which is believed to extend for 24 acres (10 hectares) about 20ft (6m) below the Georgian city. Though inspired by classical ideals, the Georgian architects were not very interested in unearthing ancient ruins. They simply built over

the top, so many mysteries still perplex the Bath Archaeological Trust. Where, for example, was the location of the *tholos* (circular temple) to which stone blocks discovered in the 19th century undoubtedly belong? (Probably, it is thought, beneath the front of the Abbey.) And where was the Roman fort and the theatre which almost certainly existed? Excavation of the Temple Precinct beneath the Pump Room in 1981–83 was a brilliant achievement, with Roman and Georgian interests both being served at once. There is an ongoing agenda for further archaeological excavations.

The economy

Tourism is crucial to Bath's economy. It provides more than 5,000 full-time jobs and contributes some £200 million each year to the local economy. The Roman Baths come fourth in Britain's league of top tourist attractions, capped only by the Tower of London, St Paul's Cathedral and Windsor Castle.

Cooling down in summer

But Bath cannot afford to rely on tourism alone. When the Ministry of Defence relocated two establishments from Bath to Bristol, it was a major blow for the city. Industry – wheel-chair manufacture, book-binding – is by necessity small scale in a city that does not lend itself to redevelopment. Future plans feature technology-based industries, which will be housed in a landscaped development on Claverton Down, close to the university (also a major employer in the city).

A book-binder at work

There are also plans to re-harness the city's oldest asset, its thermal springs. Though the city's railway station in known as 'Bath Spa', the baths haven't been used for bathing since 1976, when they were closed on health grounds, and these days guides even warn visitors against testing the water with their hands. But plans to solve such problems and reopen spa facilities (regularly mooted since the closure) may at last be realised in 1997. The baths at the top of Bath Street (the Cross Street Bath, the Hot Bath and Beau Street Bath) have been earmarked for restoration and improvements. If everything goes to plan, customers should be able to enjoy up-to-the-minute health and beauty treatments in superb 18th- and 19th-century surroundings.

Bath and the Georgians

Until the early 18th century Bath was not an elegant city. Though a popular spa, it had a mixed reputation. It was occasionally visited by royalty, but was also a magnet for the diseased poor, bogus doctors and conmen. Lodging-houses were cramped or squalid, the streets were plagued by thieves and the entertainments laid on for visitors were provincial in the extreme. The spa also had a

*Pulteney Bridge at night
and Beau Nash*

reputation for licentiousness, the act of undressing for the baths seeming to loosen more than just the ladies' whalebone stays.

The city's transformation into one of the most beautiful cities in Europe is generally attributed to the combined talents of three self-made men: Richard (Beau) Nash, a charismatic dandy; Ralph Allen, a businessman; and John Wood, a trail-blazing architect.

A key date in the city's metamorphosis was 1705 when Nash was made Master of Ceremonies by the Corporation following the death in a duel of the previous incumbent. Though a professional gambler, Nash was a born organiser with immense personal charm. On assuming his new post he took immediate measures to improve the spa's facilities, financing projects by subscriptions. He introduced street cleaning and lighting, commissioned the building of assembly rooms, and regulated the trade of the sedan chairmen, who until Nash's intervention had been operating a profitable extortion racket. He also laid down a code of behaviour for visitors. As well as banning swords, white aprons and riding boots from the new assembly rooms, it stated 'That all whisperers of lies and scandal be taken for their authors' and 'That the elder ladies and children be content with a second bench at the ball, as being past or not come to perfection' (probably coining the expression 'wall-flower').

Ralph Allen was also crucial to the meteoric rise of the West Country spa town. As well as being one of the founders of the modern post office (until Allen's reforms, the postal system was corrupt as well as inefficient) he was the first to exploit the quarries of nearby Combe Down, thus introducing the stone that was to become the city's hallmark. Allen was also a patron of the arts and invited many of the brightest minds of the day to parties at Prior

The fine art of flirting

Park, his mansion (now a National Trust property) on a hillside near Combe Down, thus adding intellectual zest to the increasingly rich Bath mix. Alexander Pope, Henry Fielding, Gainsborough, and the actors James Quin and David Garrick were among his regular guests.

The third great, and today most visible, influence on Bath was John Wood, who introduced to the city the Palladian style of architecture inspired by ancient Greece and Rome (*see page 61*). At just 23 years of age, Wood sent Allen an ambitious plan for Bath's development, in anticipation of the massive building boom that was to come. Though this was not taken up, Wood soon joined forces with the speculator Robert Gay. His first great achievement was Queen Square, begun in 1728 and finished in 1735, followed by the North and South Parades. His son, John Wood the Younger, assumed his father's mantle, transforming the Upper Town with the Royal Crescent, the Circus and the New Assembly Rooms.

The elegant environment which these men created drew the cream of fashionable society – the aristocracy and the gentry – from 1705 until the late 1750s. But the wider craze for Bath reached its zenith between 1760 and 1795, during the reign of George III (1760–1820).

Dressed for the part, c. 1745

Bath's main 'season' was September to May, with most visitors staying between six weeks and three months. From the moment the bells in Bath Abbey peeled out in welcome (the bells announced all new arrivals) to the morning their luggage was loaded on the coach for their arduous journey home, their days were a familiar round of bathing, visiting, seeing plays and attending balls. For most people, each morning began with a dip in the baths followed by a turn around the Pump Room and breakfast in the Assembly Rooms. The rest of the morning might include church and the parades, and the afternoons be divided between shops, coffee houses and gaming tables. Twice a week a ball was held at one or other of the assembly rooms. Other nights might be spent at the theatre, where during the 1770s Sarah Siddons held audiences spellbound, or at a concert given by the castrato Venanzio Rauzzini, for whom Mozart wrote *Exsultate Jubilate* in 1774. Newcomers to Bath could learn about amenities from a growing list of guidebooks to the city.

The Octagon in the Assembly Rooms

At the end of the 18th century Bath began to lose its lustre, as the upper classes deserted to Tunbridge Wells, Cheltenham and, later, breezy Brighton, where George IV had built the flamboyant Pavilion. Bath turned into a residential city favoured by the professional classes in search of a comfortable but relatively inexpensive living. Jane Austen's novel *Persuasion*, published in 1820 and partly set in Bath, depicts a city populated by colonels and captains disbanded from the Napoleonic Wars.

Jane Austen's house, 1804

Historical Highlights

5000BC Nomads hunt deer, wild pigs and ox in the area.

4000–3000BC Settlements evolve and the Avon valley is a natural conduit for the flow of ideas and trade. The oldest parts of Stonehenge date to this time.

2000–12000BC Bronze Age. Round barrow burials in surrounding area. The Monkswood Hoard, a collection of bronze items found during the construction of Monkswood Reservoir, date from the end of this period (they are displayed in the Pump Room).

1000BC Celtic peoples arrive from France and the Low Countries.

AD43 The Romans invade Britain under Emperor Claudius. In the marshy area of Bath, they find Celts worshipping a water goddess called Sulis. They name the place Aquae Sulis. Over the next 30 years they build a complex of baths and temples which draw visitors and pilgrims from far and wide. The Romans also mine lead and silver in the Mendip Hills and are the first to quarry the stone of Coombe Down, near Bath.

410 Sustained Barbarian attacks from Ireland and northern Europe force the Romans to withdraw from Britain, which now enters the Dark Ages. The bathing complex falls into disuse.

577 The Battle of Dyrham. Despite a spirited defence by the Britons, Bath is captured by the Saxons, along with Gloucester and Cirencester.

676 King Osric founds a religious establishment at Bath under Abbess Berta and pagan images are destroyed. By the 8th century, a community of monks is in charge. Under their influence, a new town rapidly evolves. Roman buildings are plundered for stone.

973 Edgar, King of all England, is crowned in Bath Abbey. The ceremony is attended by the Archbishop of Canterbury.

1066 The Norman Conquest.

1086 The Doomsday Book records that sheep are the chief livestock in Bath and the region, anticipating the medieval wool trade.

1088 John of Tours becomes Bishop of Wells, and in 1090 transfers the see to Bath where, interested in the medicinal properties of the waters, he builds a hospital. In 1192 the see is split between Bath and Glastonbury and then from 1244 between Bath and Wells.

14th century The wool and weaving industries flourish in Bath and the surrounding region (Chaucer's Wife of Bath is a weaver). They are controlled by the Church.

1499 Work begins on the present Abbey, with William Vertue, the master mason of Henry VII, engaged to work on the fan vaulting. Building is brought to a sudden halt 40 years later by the Dissolution of the Monasteries (1539).

16th century Bath regains its reputation as a spa and new baths and hospitals are built. Increasing numbers of beggars flock to Bath prompting an Act of Parliament in 1572 to restrict their number. Meanwhile the abbey is rescued from dereliction by Elizabeth I, who starts a nationwide collection.

1618–48 The Thirty Years' War damages cloth exports to Germany. Hardship among wool and clothmakers ensues. However, the industry doesn't sink yet; it turns to the home market.

1642 The Civil War between the Parliamentarians and the Royalists. Bath initially sides with the Parliamentarians but switches sides several times and eventually supports the Royalists.

1660 The monarchy is restored.

1685 Monmouth's protestant rebellion is put down.

1702 Queen Anne visits Bath to take the waters, thus accelerating a growing trend.

1706 Beau Nash becomes Master of Ceremonies and makes many improvements to the facilities at Bath, gradually transforming the town into England's most fashionable resort.

1715 The coronation of George I.

1727 The gilded bronze head of Minerva is discovered under Stall Street. It is the first clue to the Roman ruins below the Georgian city, but no further explorations are made. Around the same time Ralph Allen begins quarrying stone at Combe Down and constructs a small railway to bring the blocks into town.

1739 and 1749 Laws clamp down on gambling, one of the main pastimes in Bath, and some card games are banned. These measures have a detrimental effect on Beau Nash, who makes his living from playing cards.

1742 The General Hospital (now the Royal Mineral Hospital), intended for the visiting poor, is completed. Its instigator William Oliver becomes its chief physician.

1754–74 The Upper Town becomes increasingly fashionable. The Circus, the Royal Crescent and the Assembly Rooms are all built during this period.

1755 Building works reveal further signs of the underlying Roman baths. In 1759 more evidence – the steps of the Great Bath and part of the Gorgon's Head pediment – is found during construction of the new Pump Room.

1761 Beau Nash dies. Succeeding Masters of Ceremonies lack Nash's natural talent for the job.

1787 Plans unfold to develop the land east of Pulteney Bridge. Building work, however, is interrupted by the outbreak of war with France in 1793.

1798–9 Jane Austen writes her first novel, *Northanger Abbey*, much of which is set in Bath.

1801 Population reaches 33,000.

1810 The completion of the Kennet and Avon Canal, linking the Kennet at Newbury with the Avon at Bath, facilitates the passage of iron, stone, coal and agricultural produce between London and Bath and Bristol.

1815–16 Jane Austen writes her last novel, *Persuasion*, also set in Bath.

1832 The Great Reform Act.

1840 Brunel's Great Western Railway is brought through Bath, making access easier for visitors.

1878 Charles Davis, the city surveyor and architect, discovers Roman remains while investigating a leak from the King's Bath. Excavations reveal the full extent of the Great Bath, and further investigations uncover the Circular Bath. Tourists flock to see the amazing finds.

1925 Bath Act. New buildings must be faced with Bath stone or a suitable substitute.

1934 The Bath Preservation Trust is founded.

1942 'Baedeker raids' by the Luftwaffe in retaliation for the British bombing of the historic German cities Lübeck and Rostok. Baedeker guidebooks are reputedly used to identify appropriate targets. Many buildings are destroyed, necessitating a long programme of restoration.

1948 The prestigious International Music Festival is inaugurated.

1950s A programme to clean the blackened buildings begins. Work progresses slowly but steadily until the 1980s.

1966 Bath University is founded.

1971–80 The West Baths are excavated.

1974 Bath is incorporated in the newly created county of Avon.

1976 Spa facilities are closed on health grounds.

1981 The Temple Precinct is excavated beneath the Pump Room.

1987 Bath is designated a world heritage site by UNESCO.

1991 Bath Abbey receives a major face-lift.

1995 Plans are unveiled to restore the spa.

1996 The county of Avon is abolished. Bath and Wansdyke become a unitary council.

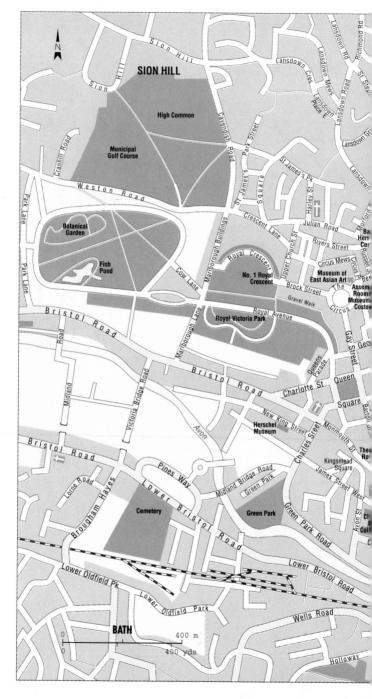

14

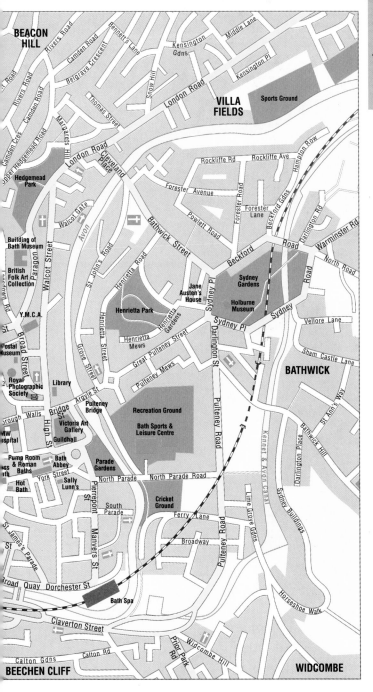

Begin at the Pump Room

Route 1

The Ancient Centre

The Pump Room – Roman Baths – Bath Abbey – Sally Lunn's

The first route focuses on the old core of Bath, the Roman Baths and the medieval Bath Abbey, finishing with a visit to the oldest house in Bath, Sally Lunn's, now a restaurant-cum-teashop with a basement museum.

Tea in the Pump Room

The ★★★ **Pump Room** ❶ (April to September daily 9am–6pm, October to March daily 9.30am–5pm, Sunday 10.30am–5pm), where this tour begins, was built between 1790–95, a replacement for an earlier, smaller pump-room. It was here that the therapeutic waters, pumped directly from the source, could be sampled in comfort. As the doctors of the day recommended taking the waters before breakfast, the Pump Room was open from 6am onwards. It was also a social arena complete with musical entertainment, though not filled with tables and chairs as it is today. In the 1800s the custom was to walk about the room to see and be seen.

Visitors today can walk along the sides of the Pump Room, but it is more pleasant to admire the room from one of the elegant tables, entertained by the Pump Room Trio (Monday to Saturday 10am–12.30pm, Sunday 3–5pm; pianist Monday to Saturday 3–5pm, Sunday 10.30am–12.30pm), with a Bath bun and coffee to hand.

At the far end of the room, a statue of Beau Nash presides over the scene, flanked by portraits of Catherine Countess of Orford and Sir Robert Walpole, Earl of Orford.

Preceding pages: The Great Bath by torchlight

Below the statue is the **Tompion clock** showing time, date and weather, donated in 1709 by Thomas Tompion, one of England's foremost clockmakers. It is a rare example of a clock with a built-in time equation showing the difference between solar (calculated by the sundial in the end window overlooking the King's Bath) and mean time. Also here are two **sedan chairs**, the main mode of transport in Georgian Bath. The one on the left, with licence plate No 68, would have been hired in the same way as taxis are today; the one topped by a coronet was a private chair.

In the alcove on the south side of the room overlooking the King's Bath, spa water is dispensed (small charge, but free to Bath residents and disabled visitors) from a lovely late 19th-century drinking fountain graced by four stone trout. If you wish to sample the water one glass is

Sample the water

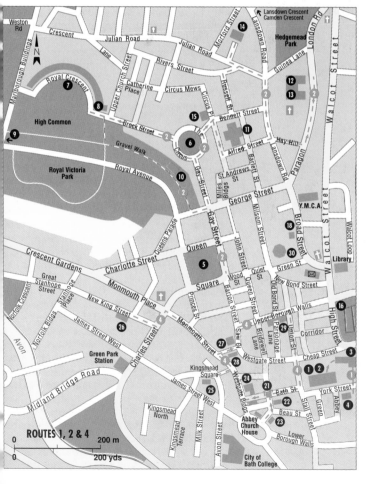

ROUTES 1, 2 & 4

Roman Bath exterior

The head of Minerva

probably sufficient to share: in Georgian times, however, as much as a gallon a day might be prescribed.

Pass through the **Sun Room** (lined with paintings and cartoons, including an oil portrait of Beau Nash by William Hoare) to the ★★★ **Roman Baths and museum** (April to September 9am–6pm, August 9am–6pm and 8–10pm, October to March 9.30am–5pm, Sunday–10.30 am–5pm). In the ticket foyer (the former Concert Hall, built at the end of the 19th century) are a number of interesting exhibits, including a bath chair, a contraption invented by James Heath in the early 19th century to replace the sedan chair. Requiring only one operator, the bath chair was cheap to run, but it could not provide the same bath-to-bed service as the sedan.

The Great Bath, seen below on entering the Roman Baths, was discovered in the 1880s by the city surveyor and architect, Charles Davis, while investigating a leak in the King's Bath that was causing hot-water floods in local cellars. The Victorians were as excited by archaeology and the past as the Georgians had been indifferent and his discovery was greeted by enormous interest throughout Britain. The colonnade and statues of Roman emperors surrounding the bath, together with the Concert Room (now the museum entrance) were added at the end of the 19th century by J. M. Brydon to appeal to the many tourists that came to see the newly exposed bath.

From here the route leads down to the heart of the Roman Baths, the **Temple Precinct**, excavated beneath the Pump Room in the early 1980s. The Temple, one of several in the vicinity, was built in around AD60, on the site of the native Sanctuary of Sulis, a Celtic goddess associated with healing, whom the Romans identified with their own goddess of healing, Minerva. Over a period of years the Romans built an elaborate religious complex complete with curative baths, whose magnificence, they hoped, would convince the native Celts of the benefits of Roman rule.

Finds from the period enliven the excavations, including votive offerings and petitions to the goddess Sulis-Minerva. Over 13,000 coins have been found here, many of them clipped to indicate that they were the property of the goddess and no longer legal tender. Curses, inscribed on pewter or lead sheets, also abound, some written backwards. These generally solicit help or revenge for mundane grievances – the theft of a glove or the heinous case of a stolen napkin ring.

Other highlights in the museum include the gilded **bronze head of Minerva**, minus crown, discovered in 1727 by workmen in Stall Street and the first intimation of the marvellous Roman ruins below Georgian Bath; the **Gorgon's head** which would have adorned the main

Temple's pediment; the corner blocks of a sacrificial altar (the figure of Hercules Bibax on the left and Bachus with a panther on the right) and the Sea Beast mosaic.

Sea Beast mosaic

The museum emerges next to the ★★ **Great Bath**, from where free guided tours leave every 15–20 minutes, taking in the East and West baths, including the medieval King's Bath. The Great Bath is the best place to see the water at close quarters. Bubbling up at a temperature of 45°C (115°F) and laden with 43 different minerals, including iron which stains the stone red, the water is thought to spring from 2 miles beneath the Mendip Hills, on which it fell as rain up to 10,000 years ago. Its green colour is caused by light reacting with algae: when the baths were roofed over, as they were in Roman times, the water would have been clear (a section of the vaulted roof is propped up against the wall at the west end of the Great Bath). The water is continually renewed. Water arrives in the northwest corner, fed from the Sacred Spring, and leaves by a sluice controlled drain.

Great Bath and sacred spring

The Great Bath was essentially a swimming bath, with the surrounding alcoves used for various beauty treatments and entertainment. The ★★ **East Baths** (excavations in progress) were for serious ablutions, offering a tepidarium (warm room), where oils and massage were applied, and a calidarium (hot room) for steaming. Hypocaust flooring would have provided heating.

19

The ★★ **West Baths** includes more of the same, plus a stoke house and the **Circular Bath**, a cold plunge bath whose waters were piped in specially (all the springs being hot). Also here is the ★★ **King's Bath**, which is overlooked by the Pump Room. In a niche on one side of the King's Bath is a statue of King Bladud, the mythical founder of Bath, who, as a prince, suffered from leprosy and roamed the countryside as a swineherd. According to the story, Bladud's ailment was miraculously cured when he stumbled upon some hot springs and plunged in. Duly rehabilitated by the court, the pearly-skinned Bladud went on to become king and found Bath on the site of the curative springs. (Myth also identifies him as the father of King Lear.) Bladud is commemorated all over the city. Even the acorns topping the pediment of the Circus are said to allude to Bladud's swineherd past.

The King's Bath was used in the Middle Ages (together with the Cross Bath and the Hot Bath (*see page 31*). It was built on the site of the Roman Sacred Spring by the Norman Bishop John of Tours, whose interest in medicine encouraged him to build an infirmary on the north side of the bath over the old Temple Precinct. The bath itself was furnished with stone seats on which the sick could wallow in the waters. The bronze rings on the sides of the bath were donated by the grateful cured.

King's Bath

From the Baths it is a short hop across Abbey Churchyard to ★★ **Bath Abbey** ❸ (suggested admission charge), the heart of Bath in the Middle Ages, when the city re-emerged from the dereliction of the Dark Ages. The introduction of Roman Catholicism by the Saxons was an important factor in Bath's renaissance. In 675 Abbess Berta founded a Convent of Holy Virgins here on land endowed by Osric, a minor Mercian king. Though there is no further record of the convent, there is evidence that a Saxon abbey existed by 781. It was here, in the abbey church, that Edgar, the first king of all England, was crowned in 973. Edgar introduced the Benedictine monks that were to control the abbey, and thus the growing medieval town, for the next 500 years.

In 1107, in the wake of the Norman conquest, the Bishop of Somerset moved the seat of the bishopric from Wells to Bath (a controversial move which eventually lead to the Pope renaming the diocese Bath and Wells) and built a Norman church on the site of the Saxon one. This lasted until 1499, when Bishop Oliver King, inspired by a dream, rebuilt the church in the late-English Gothic, or perpendicular, style characterised by flying buttresses, wide windows and fan vaulting.

The Dissolution of the Monasteries by Henry VIII in 1539 brought the work to a halt, leaving the nave without a roof. Its eventual completion is said to have come about nearly a century later after James Montague, Bishop of Bath and Wells, sought shelter here while walking in a storm with Sir John Harrington, godson of Queen Elizabeth I. According to the story, a rain-soaked Harrington turned to Montague and said, 'If the church does not keep us safe from the water above, how shall it save others from the fires below?', prompting the bishop to com-

Tomb of Bishop Montague and east view of the Abbey

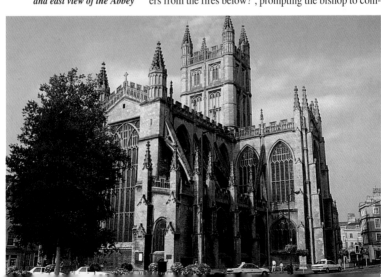

mission a roof. Records show that Queen Elizabeth I took an interest in the abbey after her visit to the city in 1574, initiating a nationwide appeal for funds.

The entrance to the abbey is through the ★ **West Front**, with its Jacob's Ladder ('the angels of God ascending and descending on it': Genesis 28: 12–17). Inside, the vast windows fill the abbey with light, earning it the epithet 'Lantern of the West' during Elizabethan times. The ★ **east window** depicts 56 scenes in the Life of Christ in brilliant stained glass. Overhead stretches the lovely ★ **fan vaulting**. This was added in two stages, the first (over the chancel) by William Vertue, master mason to Henry VII, when the abbey was built, and the rest in the mid-19th century during restorations by George Gilbert Scott that replaced Bishop Montague's lath and plaster ceiling.

Fan vaulting over the nave

One of the delights of the abbey are the ★ **memorials** to famous residents and guests who died in Bath for want of the desired cure (it is estimated that 3,879 bodies lie beneath the stone floors). Many give a vivid, sometimes tantalising, glimpse of their subject's lives, including that of a James Bassett, who 'in the Moment of Social Pleasure, received a fall, which soon deprived him of life.'

Don't miss the one dedicated to Beau Nash ('Ricardi Nash', 'Elegantiae Arbiter'). Nash died at the age of 86, impoverished and enfeebled. Nonetheless his former brilliance was recalled at his death and the corporation funded a splendid funeral. Other well-known names include Sir Isaac Pitman, the inventor of shorthand, whose memorial is adorned with a winged pen, and James Quin, whose epitaph was written by his friend David Garrick. Quin's grave, also in the abbey, bears the inscription 'The scene is changed, I am no more/Death's the last act. Now all is o'er'. For a highly readable guide to the inscriptions, buy the pamphlet *Bath Abbey Monuments* by the rector Bernard Stace, available from the Abbey's bookshop.

James Quin memorial

21

A door on the south side of the Abbey leads to the ★ **Heritage Vaults** (Monday to Saturday 10am–4pm, last admission 3.30pm, closed Sunday) tracing the history of the Abbey from Saxon times to the present day. It includes an audio presentation in which well-known British actors read extracts from letters and diaries written in Bath during its Georgian heyday.

From the abbey, the tour repairs to North Parade Passage and **Sally Lunn's** ❹, a restaurant-cum museum in the oldest house in Bath (15th century, with a 17th-century facade prettified by window boxes and olde-worlde signs). Sally Lunn's is famous for a special kind of bun (*see page 67*), which has been made on the premises since the 1680s. Its basement museum contains a 17th-century oven and archaeological finds excavated on the site.

Sally Lunn's

Route 2

The Upper Town

Queen Square – The Circus – Royal Crescent – Georgian Garden – Assembly Rooms *See map, p17*

This route is devoted to the Georgian architecture of the Upper Town, an area which became increasingly fashionable as the 18th century went on. The route takes a full day to complete, more if you want to visit all of the many museums in the area, and begins in Queen Square, a short walk northwest of the Roman Baths.

Gay Street

Quadrant of the Circus

Plane trees on Queen Square

★★ Queen Square ❺, built between 1729–39, was the first major undertaking of John Wood the Elder (*see page 61*) and was seminal to the development of the Palladian style in Bath. Its north side is especially striking, the Roman Portico uniting the terrace to palatial effect. John Wood lived on the square.

The obelisk in the centre is dedicated to Frederick Prince of Wales. It was erected by Beau Nash, in public acknowledgement of a gold enamelled snuffbox which the 'King of Bath' had received from the Prince. Gay Street, named after the landowner and speculator Robert Gay with whom Wood collaborated on several building projects in the area, rises to **★★★ The Circus ❻**, again designed by John Wood the Elder, although completed by his son. Whether inspired by the Colosseum in Rome, Stonehenge or both (a matter of conjecture), the Circus was Britain's first circular street. Note the architectural details: the acorns on the pediment, believed to allude to King Bladud (*see page 19*); the decorative frieze depicting all the arts and trades of the day; and the three types of column on the facade – Doric for the bottom storey, Ionic for the middle, and Corinthian for the top. Originally the area in the middle of the Circus, now graced by plane trees, was simply a cobbled space. Many famous people have lived on the Circus, including William Pitt the Elder (Nos 7 and 8), Clive of India (No 14) and Gainsborough (No 17).

Like his father before him, John Wood the Younger also designed an architectural first, **★★★ The Royal Crescent ❼** (1767–74), a short walk west of the Circus, along Brock Street. The Crescent is Bath's *pièce de résistance*, not least on account of its dramatic position above Royal Victoria Park, its private lawn separated from the park proper by a ha-ha. In the latter half of the 18th century the countryside became fashionable. Riding and nature rambles were introduced to the daily routine and a 'fine prospect' became desirable in homes. The meadows below the Royal Crescent were a fashionable promenade.

Comprising 30 properties, the Crescent is astonishing in its uniformity (but note the odd-man-out yellow door at No 22: *see page 6*). ★★ **No 1 Royal Crescent** ❽, the home of John Wood the Younger's father-in-law, Thomas Brock, has been turned into a museum, in which several rooms, including dining-room, study, bedroom and reception room, have been restored and furnished as they might have been in the 18th century. Printed hand-outs detail items of special interest. Note the broad landing, which allowed the sedan chairmen to turn around if they took their charges to their bedroom door.

No 1 Royal Crescent

Walking along the Royal Crescent, you will encounter several plaques recalling famous past residents including Isaac Pitman (No 17) and Elizabeth Linley (No 11). The latter was the beautiful daughter of Thomas Linley, director of music at the Assembly Rooms. A gifted soprano, she was the darling of Bath in the 1770s, painted by Gainsborough and Reynolds. Her engagement at the behest of her father to a wealthy but ageing suitor inspired *The Maid of Bath*, a satire by Samuel Foote. Eventually released from the unhappy betrothal, she went on to elope with the young and handsome playwright Richard Sheridan.

23

From the Royal Crescent **Royal Victoria Park** ❾ sweeps down to a car-park (hidden by trees) and the river. Completed in 1830 and paid for by public subscription, the park was intended to provide space and fresh-air in the increasingly built-up city. The obelisk near its eastern end records important episodes in the reign of Queen Victoria, who attended the opening of the park as an 11-year-old girl in 1830. While the park's eastern end offers bowling, tennis, putting, etc, the dells, pool, walkways and shrubberies of its ★ **Botanical Gardens** conceal many delights – lichen-covered statues, a copy of the Temple of Minerva, a sundial, a dovecote and more.

In the Botanical Gardens and bowling in the park

Georgian Garden

Captain Wade, Master of Ceremonies from 1769–77

Chandelier in the Ball Room

At the other end of the scale from Royal Victoria Park is the ★ **Georgian Garden** ❿ (May 1 to October 31 Monday to Friday 9am–4pm, closed weekends and Bank Holidays, free admission), off the Gravel Walk below the Royal Crescent. Excavations in 1985 to restore this walled garden to its 18th-century state revealed original paths and flowerbeds. Planted with species typical during the 1760s, it is restful in its symmetry and privacy.

One of the key ingredients of the Upper Town in Georgian times was the ★★★ **Assembly Rooms** ⓫ (10am–5pm, Sunday 11pm–5pm; free admission), located in Bennett Street, on the east side of the Circus. These rooms were one of three sets in the town, the others being Harrison's (later Simpson's) and Lindsey's (later Wiltshire's) in the lower town. As the century went on there was some friction between the upper and lower assemblies, and from 1777 they each had their own master of ceremonies. These Rooms, the only ones still standing, were designed by John Wood the Younger in 1769. The necessary £20,000 was raised by 'tontine' subscriptions, whereby the shares of any shareholder who died were split between remaining members. Running costs and profits were met by subscriptions. One guinea allowed up to three people to attend the season's balls, but it was necessary to take out additional subscriptions to attend concerts or to play cards.

The Rooms comprise a **ballroom**, the largest 18th-century building in Bath at 106ft (32m) long, the **Octagon**, a **Card Room** and a **Tea Room**. The ballroom is magnificent, graced by five cut-glass chandeliers. The plain area below the Corinthian columns around the wall was taken up by tiers of seating, with the front row reserved for the belles of the ball and the rear for the plain or elderly.

A ball was held once a week, beginning at 6pm with the highest ranking lady present being led onto the floor for a minuet. Minuets went on until 8pm when the more energetic country dances commenced. At 9pm tea was taken, followed by more dancing until 11 o'clock. During this time non-dancers and others could play cards in the Octagon or, when it was added to the complex in 1777, the Card Room. Gambling was a major part of life in Georgian Bath. Nash actually made his living from it, and laws curtailing gambling in 1739 and 1745 contributed to his eventual decline.

As the century wore on private parties were preferred over public balls. In 1801 Jane Austen, then living in Bath, wrote to her sister Cassandra: 'After tea we cheered up; the breaking up of private parties sent some scores more to the Ball, and tho' it was shockingly and inhumanly thin for this place, there were people enough I suppose to have made five or six very pretty Basingstoke assemblies.'

Dancing a minuet in the Tea Room

In the 19th century the Upper Rooms gradually declined, though not without flashes of their former glory when Johann Strauss and Franz List performed and Charles Dickens gave public readings. In 1920 the rooms were converted into a cinema, and though restored in 1931 when the National Trust acquired them they were badly bombed during the Baedeker raids of 1942 (*see page 11*). Since then they have been steadily restored, culminating in a final push in 1991 costing £3 million.

Downstairs is the ★ **Museum of Costume** (Monday to Saturday 10am–5pm, Sunday 11am–5pm). Free guided tours lasting 30 minutes and leaving from the Octagon, show how the fashions of the last four centuries have reflected their times: how powdered wigs suddenly went out of fashion in the 1790s when a new tax on powder was introduced to raise money for the brewing war with France; how sober muslins, the opposite of the rich silk brocades of the 1760s, became fashionable daywear in the wake of the French Revolution as signs of wealth were concealed for fear of social rebellion. Though the museum covers fashion from the 16th century to the present day, it is the insights into Georgian society that are most fascinating. We learn that, while men generally wore wigs, women would supplement their own hair with false hair and padding and then hold it all in place with perfumed fat, perhaps washing it twice a year. As a result, it was quite usual for a woman to carry a head scratcher, which she would used whenever the urge took her, even at a concert or a ball.

Coat from 1894, Museum of Costume

Leaving the Assembly Rooms, turn left and then left again into **Alfred Street** where, at No 14, you can see a full complement of original Georgian ironwork framing the entrance. It includes the horn-shaped snuffers where sedan chairmen could extinguish their rag torches (links), a boot scrape, and a winch which would deliver heavy goods such as wines to the cellar. Though the ironwork is painted black, as it is all over Bath today, in the 18th century it might have been painted grey, green or even bright blue, as the Building of Bath Museum points out (*see below*).

At the end of Alfred Street, Lansdown Road leads to two handsome crescents, first the incomplete Camden Crescent, designed by John Eveleigh in 1788, and eventually Lansdown Crescent, designed by John Palmer in 1789. By turning down Hay Hill, however, you reach the Paragon. It was at No 1 the Paragon that Jane Austen stayed on her first visit to Bath in 1797. The buildings flanking the near side of the road are known as the Vineyards, on account of the vines which flourished here until the land was developed in the 1760s.

The Countess of Huntingdon's Chapel

A left turn here will take you to the **Countess of Huntingdon's Chapel** with its picturesque Gothic windows and battlemented breastwork, which houses the Building of Bath Museum and the British Folk Art Collection. Selina, Countess of Huntingdon (1707–91) was an aristocratic Methodist, who sold her jewels to raise money for the cause. This was the fourth chapel that she built. John Wesley preached here on a number of occasions, 'attacking the devil in his own headquarters,' as he saw it, and drew surprisingly large audiences. The presence of the Countess in Bath placed Nash in a social quandary. Though he disliked the Methodists, and had several run-ins with them, his natural snobbery demanded deference to the aristocracy. In the end, an encounter with the Countess in which she persuaded him to listen to a sermon by the zealot George Whitfield restored his animosity to the full.

British Folk Art Collection

The ★★ **Building of Bath Museum** 🄬 (Tuesday to Sunday and Bank Holidays 10.30am–5pm, closed Mondays and 11 December to 29 February) is an illuminat-

ng account of the talents and techniques that created the lovely, seamless facades of Bath. Every aspect of building is covered, from the speculative deals that drove the building boom to the evolution of modern paints and wallpapers. Outside, a block of Bath stone invites you to test its properties with a saw.

Across the courtyard of the chapel is the charming **British Folk Art Collection** 13 (Tuesday to Saturday and Bank Holidays 10.30am–5pm, Sundays April to October only 2–5pm), devoted to the art and crafts of ordinary people in the 18th and 19th centuries. Its attached shop is a good place to find unusual presents.

One of the most interesting museums in the Upper Town is the ★ **Bath Heritage Centre** 14 (Easter to October daily 10am–5pm, November to Easter weekends only 10am–5pm; return to Lansdown Road by cutting left past the Bath Antiques Market, then take Julian Road to Christ Church). Based upon 'the Bowler Collection', the eclectic contents of a 19th-century brass foundry and soda water manufactory, the museum is a real antidote to the giddy Georgian world of baths and balls.

Bath Heritage Centre

Jonathan Burdett Bowler was the archetypal small businessman, who built-up his engineering business through hard work and careful management. He appears to have adhered to two simple maxims: 'never throw anything away that might come in handy', and 'no job too large or small'. Bowler would turn his hand to anything to meet customer demand, and in 1877 diversified into the manufacture and distribution of soda water using Bath's famous springs. Most of his 15 children worked for the family firm at some stage, though this didn't stop it from eventually closing in 1969, nearly a century after it opened. The 19th-century store, engine room, workshops, office and soda factory have been reassembled here, uprooted from their original site in Corn Street in the lower town. A guide adds insight to the exhibits and invites you to guess the purpose of mysterious-looking objects: a lady's suspender? a pair of sugar tongs? An old-fashioned café upstairs offers inexpensive refreshments, but not, sadly any of JBB's Noted Bath Waters, such as Orange Champagne and Horsehound Beer.

Exhibit in the Museum of East Asian Art

From the museum, Russell Street leads back to Bennet Street and the Assembly Rooms. As you pass Circus Place, note the **Museum of East Asian Art** 15 (April to October 10am–6pm, Sunday 10am–5pm, November to March 10am–5pm, Sunday noon–5pm), containing an exquisite collection of Eastern Antiquities acquired by lawyer Brian S. McElney during his working life in Hong Kong. From here, Gay Street will deliver you back to where this tour began.

Route 3

Across Pulteney Bridge

Guildhall – Victoria Art Gallery – Pulteney Bridge - Great Pulteney Street – Holburne Museum – Sydney Gardens

Concentrating on the area east of the centre, this tour crosses the River Avon to Bathwick, an area free from development until the Pulteney Bridge linked it to the city centre in the 1770s. It begins, however, at the Guildhall on the west side of the bridge, just behind Bath Abbey which symbolises the growing power and wealth of the mercantile classes during the late 1700s.

Banqueting Hall

The **Guildhall** ⑯ was designed in the new Adam style (*see page 63*) in the late 1770s by Thomas Baldwin to replace an earlier edition of 1625 (on a different site), though the wings topped by decorative cupolas were added by John Brydon over a century later in 1891. Baldwin was in his early 20s at the time, but his design was widely admired and he went on to become the city architect. Its ★★ **Banqueting Hall** and ante-rooms (open to visitors providing no functions are in progress), intended as 'assembly rooms' for the aldermen and their guests, rivalled the more exclusive Upper and Lower rooms in their magnificence. Portraits of famous Bath figures surround the large portrait of George III ('mad George') by the studio of Joshua Reynolds. Over one of the fireplaces is a portrait of Ralph Allen (*see below*), by William Hoare. The chandeliers, the finest in Bath, were made in 1778 by William Parker.

Atop the Victoria Art Gallery

Next door to the Guildhall is the entrance to the **covered market** (added in 1895), a lively cut-through to the Grand Parade, and then the **Victoria Art Gallery** ⑰ (Monday to Friday 10am–5.30pm, Saturday 10am–5pm, closed Sunday) whose collection of paintings on the first floor includes Turner's *West Front of Bath Abbey*, *Adoration of the Magi*, attributed to Hugo Van der Goes, portraits by Zoffany and Gainsborough, several Sickerts and a Whistler. (Entrance to the museum is on Bridge Street.)

Bath Postal Museum

From here the High Street rises to Northgate Street, beyond which, in Broad Street, is the **Bath Postal Museum** ⑱ (April to October Monday to Saturday 11am–5pm, Sunday 2–5pm) from where the world's first postage stamp, the Penny Black, was sent on 2 May 1840. Bath played a pivotal role in the development of the British postal system, thanks to Ralph Allen, who expanded established routes and stamped out corruption, and John Palmer, who improved efficiency by the introduction of ail coaches which were not required to stop at toll-gates. 1784, the run from Bristol to London took just 14 hours.

Exhibits track the history of the postal service, but also ouch upon some delightful peripheral topics – a collec- on of early valentines covered in cupids and cute Vic- priana and an 'address cabinet' of famous Bath residents, omplete with portraits and biographical notes.

Pulteney Bridge

ridge Street leads on to ★★ **Pulteney Bridge**, first pass- ng on the right the Grand Parade leading down to the arade Gardens (admission charge) and thence the North nd South parades (both designed by John Wood the El- er). Grand Parade (a Victorian addition) remains popu- ar today, offering picture-postcard views of Pulteney ridge and the weir. Though this is a recent model (1971), weir has existed here since the Middle Ages, when it robably worked the woollen mills.

Commissioned by William Johnstone Pulteney and de- igned by Robert Adam between 1770 and 1774, Pulteney ridge, a mini Pontevechio, cost an astonishing £11,000 o build, not least on account of the tiny shops lining both ides. The bridge paved the way for the development of athwick, a virgin estate owned by Pulteney, under the di- ection of the young Thomas Baldwin, architect of the new uildhall (*see page 28*). The south side of Pulteney Bridge vas restored to its original glory in 1975, when out- uildings defacing its flat front were demolished; the back, owever, which is visible from the Podium shopping entre or from the river, is still overhung with back kitchens nd store rooms. On the right side of the bridge, steps lead own to the Avon, where river cruises depart for Bathamp- on weir from the landing stage every hour or so, and river- ank walks lead to North Parade Bridge (stairs in the ollhouses offer access to the road). A tiny café below ulteney Bridge doubles as a puppet theatre, which is a ig hit with children.

29

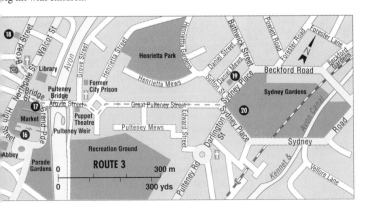

Pulteney Bridge leads into Argyle Street, off whic Grove Street contains the former **City Prison**, built b Thomas Atwood in Palladian style in 1773 and now turne into flats. On the corner of Argyle and Grove streets not a *trompe l'oeil* advertising the 'George Gregory Booksho and Lending Library' in a first-floor window.

From Laura Place ★★**Great Pulteney Street** sweep down to the Holburne Museum. This imposing street wa designed by Thomas Baldwin in the late 1780s, incorpo rating some elements of a previous design by Rober Adam, Pulteney's original choice of architect. Baldwi stepped into Adam's shoes following Pulteney's death when Henrietta Pulteney assumed control of the projec and needed to curb mounting expenses. The Bathwick pro ject was interrupted by the economic slump of the 1790 and the huge array of crescents and terraces that Bald win envisaged fanning out from Great Pulteney Street wa never fully realised. The street, the widest in Bath at 100f (30m), was a fashionable address in the late 18th and earl 19th centuries, as the many plaques testify. Willian Wilberforce (1759–1833) stayed at No 36; Emma Hamil ton at No 72; Thomas Baldwin himself lived at No 6. Alsc here are two examples of the six-sided letter-boxes known as Penfold boxes (after their designer J.W. Penfold), use briefly in the mid-19th century until faults in the hexag onal design were found to trap letters.

Looking down Great Pulteney Street

Great Pulteney Street features in Jane Austen's *North anger Abbey* and *Persuasion*. Austen herself lived at No 4 Sydney Place ⓳ between 1801 and 1804, and Queer Charlotte Sophia, consul to George III, lodged for a while at 103 Sydney Place. **Sydney Gardens** are frequently mentioned in Jane Austen's letters, as a place for public breakfasts, galas and fireworks. In the 19th century they were used for balloon ascents. Dissecting the gardens are Brunel's Great Western Railway (1840–41) and the Ken-net and Avon Canal (opened 1810), industrial additions that were elegantly incorporated by means of landscaped cuttings and pretty stone and cast-iron bridges. Other at-tractions include a mock Roman temple.

Jane Austen's house

Sydney Gardens

The **Holburne Museum** ⓴, on the edge of the gar-dens, was originally the Sydney Hotel. The museum (Mon-day to Saturday 11am–5pm, Sunday 2.30–5.30pm), based upon the collection of Sir Thomas Holburne (1793–1874), is devoted to decorative and fine art of the 17th and 18th centuries, including paintings, silver, porcelain, minia-tures, glass and furniture. Among the paintings are works by Turner, Stubbs, Gainsborough and Reynolds. Gains-borough made his name in Bath, painting the portraits of famous figures and aristocrats. His rapid success can be gauged by his escalating fees, beginning at a modest 5 guineas in 1760 and rising to 100 guineas in around 1774.

Route 4

West of the Roman Baths

Cross Bath – St John's Hospital – Herschel Museum – Theatre Royal – Royal Mineral Water Hospital *See map, p17*

This route is devoted to the area west of the Roman Baths, earmarked to form the centre of the restored spa planned for 1997 (*see page 7*). It puts special emphasis on the city's strong medical and theatrical associations, and pays tribute to William Herschel, an amateur astronomer who discovered Uranus in 1781.

A few metres west of the Pump Room, along colonnaded Bath Street (designed by Thomas Baldwin in 1791), the ★ **Cross Bath** ㉑ seems miles away from the buskers and crowds in Abbey Churchyard. Restored by the Springs Foundation, this bath, with its curvaceous lines and delicate carvings, is an oasis of tranquillity, befitting its long associations with healing. During the 17th century the bath had a reputation for curing sterility. Mary of Modena, the wife of James II, conceived a much-needed heir (later the Old Pretender) after bathing here.

Bath Street Colonnade and Cross Bath

31

A succession of baths have been built on this spot, below which the coolest of Bath's three hot springs rises. The current building was begun by Thomas Baldwin in 1791 and completed by John Palmer. Close by is the **Hot Bath** ㉒ (also known as the Old Royal Hetling Bath), so far unrestored, which was built by John Wood the Younger in 1773 in a plain, angular style. This bath was fed by the hottest spring (48°C/118°F), which also served an adjacent 'lepers' bath' for people with skin diseases. In the early 19th century a swimming pool was added to the Hot Bath to upgrade the facility to Continental standards. Note the sign advertising Hetling Pump Room on the wall opposite the west side portico. On the corner of Beau Street and Hot Bath Street you can dip into the ★ **Hot Baths Gallery** ㉓ (Monday to Saturday 10am–4pm) to refresh your senses with contemporary art and design.

Returning to the north side of the Cross Bath, a path leads between the buildings of the **Hospital of St John the Baptist** ㉔, founded in 1174 by Bishop Reginald Fitzjocelin. St John's was one of several charitable hospitals built here during the Middle Ages, a trend begun in the 12th century by the Norman bishop John of Tours, a believer in the benefits of curative baths. Modern opinion believes many ailments had their origins in lead poisoning. Lead had many different uses at the time; it was even used as a fungicide in port wine.

Hot Baths Gallery

On Kingsmead Square

The Herschel Museum

32

Westgate Buildings lead up to Kingsmead Square. Here Avon Street, a slum area during Victorian times and heavily bombed during the Baedeker Raids of 1942, runs south through post-war development to the river. On the square is **Rosewell House** ㉕, built in 1735 by John Strahan of Bristol for Thomas Rosewell. Though baroque architecture dominated continental cities in the 17th and early 18th century, this is the only baroque building in Bath.

Out on a limb, in New King Street (No 19), is the **Herschel Museum** ㉖ (March to October 2–5pm, November to February Saturday and Sunday only), the house and observatory of William Herschel. Herschel came to Bath from Hanover in 1761 to take up a position as organist at the Octagon Chapel on Milsom Street and later succeeded Thomas Linley as musical director of the Assembly Rooms. But his abiding love was star-gazing and he would hurry home from concerts to roam through the skies with the help of home-made telescopes and his devoted sister Caroline. It was from the garden of this house that he discovered Uranus in 1781, adding to the number of known planets for the first time since antiquity. Following his discovery, Herschel was made Director of the Royal Astronomical Observatory. The museum documents Herschel's two careers. In the basement is the workshop where he built his telescopes.

Back at Kingsmead Square, Saw Close runs up to the **Theatre Royal** ㉗, one-time home of Beau Nash and the hub of Bath's thriving theatre scene from 1805, when the hitherto renowned Orchard Street Theatre moved here. Orchard Street was associated with some of the finest actors of the day, including James Quin, David Garrick and Sarah Siddons. The city also drew dramatists who set their plays in Bath – invariably farces pivoting on the collision of town and country manners and peopled by cocky servants, rakes and fops. Richard Sheridan joined his family in Bath in 1771, but made his name in London with *The Rivals*, a satire set in Bath (which his friend Frederick Reynolds mocked in *The Dramatist*, also set in Bath*)*. In Bath, Sheridan was famous for eloping with Elizabeth Linley, daughter of Thomas Linley and inspiration for Samuel Foote's play *The Maid of Bath*. It is worth trying to see a performance at the theatre. Its entrance on Saw Close leads to swagged and gilded tiers of plush red velvet. Back-stage tours are available.

Next to the theatre is the house (now Lord Baggot's Dining Room) in which Beau Nash died in 1761 tended by his mistress Juliana Papjoy. He lived here (next door to the home he occupied during the height of his success) for the last 16 years of his life, surviving on a small pension of

Theatre Royal interior

£10 a month. On the other side of the theatre is **Seven Dials** , a modern complex of shops and restaurants. Handprints of actors and actresses, including John Gielgud, Michael Hordern and Derek Jacobi are cast in bronze around the fountain in the central courtyard.

Derek Jacobi's hands

From here, Barton Street leads up to Queen Square, the start of Route 2 (*see page 22*), and Upper Borough Walls leads to the Royal Mineral Water Hospital, with a glimpse on the way of **Trim Bridge**, containing the first 18th-century development outside the city walls and spanned by St John's Gate. **The Royal Mineral Water Hospital** was a philanthropic venture built on the site of a theatre by John Wood the Elder between 1738 and 1742, under the collective auspices of Dr William Oliver of Bath Oliver fame, who had long dreamed of a new charitable hospital for the deserving poor, Ralph Allen, who provided the stone, and Beau Nash, who raised funds for the project. Ongoing expenses were met from the revenue obtained through fines on illegal gambling and collections at church services. William Oliver, a fervent believer in the efficacy of mineral baths, and author of *A Practical Essay on the Use and Abuse of Warm Bathing in Gouty Cases* (1751), appointed himself physician to the hospital. The hospital is still in use as the Royal National Hospital for Rheumatic Diseases.

33

Directly in front of the hospital Old Bond Street leads up to Milsom Street, laid out in the 1760s and a famous shopping thoroughfare since Jane Austen's time. Among its chic shops is the **Octagon Chapel**, now the headquarters for the **Royal Photographic Society**, which was designed by Thomas Lightholer in 1767 as a propiretary (subscription) chapel with fireplaces, carpets and 'every accommodation of ease and refinement'. Union Street, also good for shopping, leads back to Stall Street and the Pump Room, where this route began.

Milsom Street

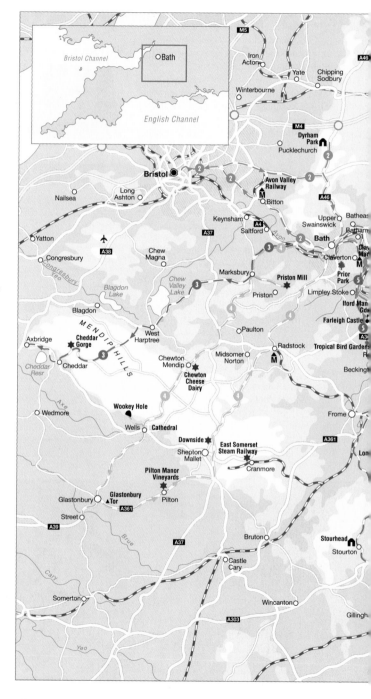

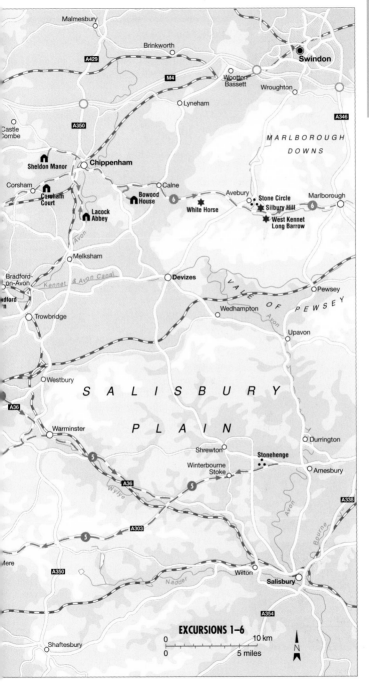

Malmesbury

Brinkworth

Swindon

Wootten
Bassett

Wroughton

A346

Lyneham

MARLBOROUGH

DOWNS

Castle
Combe

A350

A429

Sheldon Manor

Chippenham

M4

Calne

6

Avebury

Stone Circle

Marlborough

Corsham

Bowood
House

White Horse

Silbury Hill

6

Corsham
Court

Lacock
Abbey

West Kennet
Long Barrow

Avon

Melksham

Bradford-
on-Avon

Kennet & Avon Canal

Devizes

VALE

Pewsey

adford
n

Trowbridge

Wedhampton

OF

PEWSEY

Avon

Upavon

Westbury

S A L I S B U R Y

A36

Warminster

P L A I N

Durrington

5

Shrewton

Stonehenge

Winterbourne
Stoke

Amesbury

A36

5

Wylye

A338

5

A303

Avon

Bourne

Mere

A350

Naddel

Wilton

Salisbury

A354

Shaftesbury

EXCURSIONS 1–6

0   10 km

0   5 miles

N

Local face in Bradford-on-Avon

Excursion 1

Bradford-on-Avon

American Museum – Bradford-on-Avon – Iford Manor Gardens – Farleigh Hungerford Castle *See map, p34–.*

The former mill town of Bradford-on-Avon lies just 8 miles (13km) from Bath. It offers a picturesque riverside location, a rich industrial heritage, one of the best Saxon churches in the country and a 14th-century tithe barn. Though the distance is short, the route described here, which also takes in the highly recommended American Museum and Iford Manor Gardens, is likely to take a full day to complete. It is designed with car drivers in mind, but both the American Museum and Bradford-on-Avon are easily reached by public transport (for the museum, take bus No 18, and for Bradford-on-Avon Nos 265 or X4, departing from the bus station). Drivers should leave Bath on the A36 bypassing Bathampton (home and burial place of Sickert, two of whose paintings are in the Victoria Art Gallery in Bath), turning right for the American Museum (signposted) after 3 miles (5km).

Occupying neoclassical Claverton Manor (1820) on Claverton Down, the ★★ **American Museum** (25 March to 5 November Tuesday to Sunday 2–5pm, Bank Holiday Sundays and Mondays 11–5pm, Mondays in August 2–5pm) offers an absorbing picture of American domestic life between the 17th and 19th centuries. The attention to detail, and the charming and informative women who staff the museum, make this one of the most satisfying museums in the region.

Claverton Manor

A series of rooms have been furnished according to various eras and areas, a number of them shipped from the USA and reassembled. There are some 12 interiors altogether (plus smaller reconstructions), ranging from the 17th-century Keeping Room to the elegant 18th-century 'Deer Park Parlour' from Maryland, the Stencilled Bedchamber (c1830), and the 'Greek Revival Room', based on a New York dining room c1824–35. The New Orleans Bedroom, with its blood-red wall-paper, ornate Louis XV-style half-tester bed, dressing table and love seat, evokes the ante-bellum world of the young Scarlett O'Hara. In addition, there are displays documenting westward expansion, whaling, the history of the North American Indian, and American arts and crafts such as quilting, Indian beading and Shaker furniture-making.

The American theme extends to the manor's grounds, with a replica of George Washington's rose and flower garden at Mount Vernon, complete with a copy of the oc-

Just like Mount Vernon

tagonal garden house that served as a school for the president's step-grandchildren; a colonial herb garden and shop, where you can buy a 'tussie-mussie', traditionally carried by young ladies on their way to church; a teepee; and a 'milliner's shop', a summerhouse containing a collection of decorated bandboxes. A gallery of American Folk Art occupies the former stables. Visit the tea-room for real American cookies.

Leaving the American Museum, turn right at the A36 and then, just before Limpley Stoke, left along the B3108 to ★★ **Bradford-on-Avon**.

The history of this scenic town on the Avon is rooted in the woollen industry, which flourished throughout the region during the late Middle Ages, evolving from a simple trade in wool to a cottage-based weaving industry. In the 18th century it was factory based and specialised machinery was introduced, but the industry was already in decline, squeezed by competition from towns in northern England, including Bradford in Yorkshire. It lasted until the mid to late 19th century, by which time the rubber industry was beginning to take over thanks to Stephen Moulton, a manufacturer of rubberised clothing, who secured an order to supply soldiers in the Crimean War. Evidence of the wool and cloth industry are everywhere in Bradford: weavers' cottages, the mills flanking the river, the decorated merchants' houses. The town also has a large number of non-conformist chapels. John Wesley preached here and the tireless Countess of Huntingdon (*see page 26*) was active.

The focal point of the town is the main **bridge** (a 17th-century remodelling of a 13th-century original), crossing the 'broad ford' which gives the town its name and offering a picture-postcard view of the town piled upon

*Georgian townhouses
and the Bridge*

Bridge Tea Rooms and interior of the Saxon church

the hill behind; fine Georgian townhouses blend harmoniously with 16th-century weavers' cottages. In the middle of the bridge is a 'chapel', actually a 17th-century lock-up for miscreants (though the 13th-century bridge may have included a chapel for pilgrims on their way to Glastonbury). At the foot of the bridge are the photogenic Bridge Tea Rooms, a perfect image for the lid of a chocolate box.

Off Market Street, Church Street leads to the Saxon ★ **church of St Laurence**, founded by St Adhelm in around 700 but rebuilt around 1001, with carved angels over the chancel arch. St Laurence was recovered from secular use (part school from 1715, and part cottage) in around 1871, 15 years after the vicar, an amateur archaeologist, discovered the two carved angels. Close to St Laurence is the Norman parish church.

Back on Market Street, the Shambles, site of the medieval market, leads off to the right, and at the top of the street is Priory Barn belonging to the manor from which the porch in the garden at Corsham Court (*see page 55*) originally belonged. The Methuen family of Corsham were leading players in the wool industry in Bradford. A memorial to Thomas Methuen (1684–1733) can be found in the parish church here, along with other memorials to Bradford cloth merchants.

Signposted off the Frome road on the edge of town is the ★ **Bradford Barn**, an early 14th-century tithe barn. Tithes, a 'tenth' of the agricultural produce of a parish paid as a kind of tax to the Church, were first introduced by King Offa of Mercia in the 8th century. This particular barn would also have been used for storing the produce of the Abbess of Shaftesbury's estate, to which Bradford belonged. From here, a gentle walk of about 2 miles (3km) along the towpath of the Kennet and Avon canal leads to the pretty village of Avoncliff. Alternatively, bikes can be hired by the day, half-day or hour from Lock Inn Cottage, off the Frome road (*see page 71*).

Iford Manor Gardens

Leaving Bradford by the Frome road (the B3109), you can visit the Italianate **Iford Manor Gardens** (April and October, Sundays and Easter 2–5pm, May to September 2–5pm, closed Monday and Friday), designed by the Edwardian architect and landscape gardener Harold Peto, who once lived here.

The exit from the gardens leads to the A36, where a right turn will deliver you back to Bath. Alternatively, a left turn leads to the junction with the A366 to Trowbridge, off which is **Farleigh Hungerford Castle** (English Heritage) dating from the late 14th century (1 April to 30 September 10am–6pm, 1 to 31 October 10am–4pm, 1 November to 31 March Wednesday to Sunday 10am–4pm).

Excursion 2

Bristol

Bristol – Dyrham Park *See map, p34–5*

While Bath is primarily a city of pleasure, Bristol (population: 399,600), just 13 miles (21km) away, is a city of industry. For 300 years a major British port, second only to London, Bristol was – and still is to a lesser extent – the West Country's window on the world and its main magnet for labour. But Bristol's industrial character doesn't mean it has nothing to interest visitors. Important since Saxon times – and a port of call for Phoenician traders long before that – the city has a rich and varied history plus an attractive setting afforded by the cliffs of the Avon. With seagulls wheeling overhead and salty breezes off the Bristol Channel, it makes an invigorating change from cosy, compact Bath.

Bristol Temple Meads

There are two direct roads to Bristol from Bath, the A4 and the A431 (the latter passing Avon Valley Railway steam train museum at Bitton). Alternatively, regular trains leave from Bath to Bristol Temple Meads. The Tourist Information Centre in Bristol (free maps) is located in St Nicholas Street close to Bristol Bridge.

This walking tour of Bristol begins at the cathedral on College Green, uphill from The Centre.

★★ **Bristol Cathedral** was originally the church of an Augustinian abbey founded in around 1140 by Robert Fitzardinge. When the abbey was closed following the dissolution of the monasteries in 1539, the church was also closed and the still unfinished nave was demolished. It was reopened as a cathedral in 1542, but building

The cathedral's nave

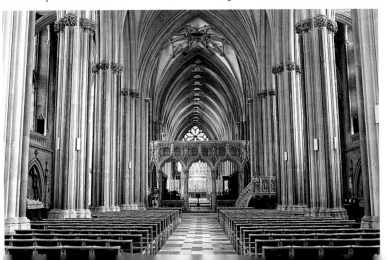

works (including replacement of the nave) were not completed until the 19th and 20th centuries. It is a rare example of a hall church, in which the roof is at the same height throughout the building. This makes it extremely strong. Though Bristol was heavily bombed during World War II, the cathedral escaped relatively lightly.

The tour of the interior leads in a clockwise direction. The original unfinished **nave** was demolished after the dissolution, resulting in a truncated church right up until the mid-19th century. This nave was eventually added in 1868–77 by George Edmund Street. At the **crossing**, an upward glance to the right will alight on variously decorated and coloured bosses in the vaulting of the south transept, added in the 15th century.

Elder Lady Chapel

The **Elder Lady Chapel** (1220) contains some fine naturalistic carvings of animals, including monkeys, which link it to the stone mason who worked on Wells cathedral, where similar carvings are found.

Unlike the nave, the **choir** (1298–1330) has lierne-rib vaulting, the earliest of its kind in England. The stalls have some finely carved misericords (ingenious props on the underside of the hinged seats); needlepoint cushions mirror the scenes depicted in the carvings.

The **Eastern Lady Chapel** (1298), behind the High Altar, is especially interesting for its deep green, blue, red and gold paintwork (partially restored in 1935). Medieval

Eastern Lady Chapel

cathedrals would have been covered in such colours, creating a very different impression from the one of muted stone offset by stained glass that we get today. The heraldry on the screen and around the edge of the east window relates to the Berkeley family, descendants of the founder of the abbey, to whom this chapel was originally going to be dedicated, and family effigies stand above the shields. The parapet was given by one of the last abbots, Abbot Burton (1526–30), who is represented by a rebus (visual pun): a thistle (for Bur) and a barrel (for ton). Several of the 15th-century abbots are represented by effigies in the star-shaped alcoves around the walls.

As you turn into the south aisle, a doorway leads into the sacristy and **Berkeley Chapel,** the former containing windows filled with fragments of early stained glass and framed by charming stone carvings of foliage (including a snail). In the left-hand niche of the sacristy is a flue which would have carried off the smoke from the oven where bread for the Eucharist was baked. The Berkeley Chapel is a chantry chapel, built in remembrance of Lady Berkeley in 1337.

Further up the south aisle is a chapel to the Newton family, past which is the entrance to the Chapter House and Cloisters. As you turn towards these, note, on the left, the Saxon stone sculpture (c.1050) depicting the

Harrowing of Hell (a just discernible Christ trampling Satan while comforting a pregnant woman), one of the most important pieces of Saxon sculpture in England.

The Norman **Chapter House** (1150) was the scene of social unrest in 1831, when rioters threatened to burn down the cathedral. Afterwards the east wall had to be rebuilt. It has unusual zigzag decoration and seating for 40.

From the cathedral, Park Street rises to Bristol University and the City Museum and Art Gallery, passing en route Great George Street (off to the left) containing the late 18th-century ★ **Georgian House** (Tuesday to Saturday 10am–1pm and 2–5pm), a museum to 18th-century life and said to be where Wordsworth first met Coleridge in 1795. It was a Bristol company, Biggs and Cottle that first printed *Lyrical Ballads* (1798). At the very top of Park Street, Queen's Road leads off to **Clifton Village**, where Brunel's impressive ★**suspension bridge** spans the gorge and the city's smart set live and shop.

Downhill from the cathedral, Denmark street, left off The Centre, leads to **Harvey's**, the company behind world-famous Harvey's Bristol Cream sherry produced in Jerez de la Frontera in southwest Spain. The cellar museum (Monday to Friday 10am–1pm and 2–5pm, Saturday 10am–5pm) documents the history of Harvey's since its founding in 1796 and the tradition of importing wines though Bristol since the Middle Ages, when it was traded for cloth and corn. It covers all angles of the trade and throws up some interesting facts. How, for example, sales of Bristol Cream soared in the 1930s through advertising aimed at women keen to be at the forefront of fashion by holding a sherry party. Admission to the museum includes a glass of Harvey's Bristol Cream with ice.

Harvey's museum

41

From here, return to The Centre and head for the **Watershed**, a complex of shops, bars and restaurants on a finger of the Floating Harbour (created in 1810 as a non-tidal dock), from where, beneath Neptune's statue, ferries leave for the *SS Great Britain* (and to other landing stages) every 40 minutes or so. Alternatively, the ship can be reached on foot (walk along Narrow Quay, past the Arnolfini Arts Complex, and cross Prince Street Bridge, where a right turn leads along the south side of the Floating Harbour).

The Watershed

★ *SS Great Britain* (summer 10am–6pm, winter 10am–5pm) represents Bristol's glorious heyday as a major shipbuilding centre, which inspired the expression 'ship-shape and Bristol fashion'. First floated in 1843, it was the first propeller-driven iron ocean-going ship in history and was intended to wipe out the lead that America had gained in transatlantic passenger shipping in the previous 30 years. Designed by Isambard Kingdom Brunel, chief engineer of the Great Western Steamship

SS Great Britain

Company, the vessel measured 322ft (98m) in length, had a gross tonnage of 2,936, and was fitted with six masts for use when the wind was favourable in order to save coal. As well as surpassing other ships in terms of speed and capacity, it set new standards of comfort.

But the *Great Britain*'s career was not without mishap. In 1946, the year after its first voyage, the captain grounded the ship in Dundrum Bay off Ireland, where it was to stay for almost a year. Attempts at refloating and the cost of repairs bankrupted the Great Western Steamship Company. Bought by Gibbs, Bright and Company of Liverpool, the *Great Britain* was substantially altered for its relaunch in 1852, after which it spent 24 years transporting emigrants to Australia. It is estimated that some 250,000 Australians are descended from its passengers.

The ship, which was recovered from the Falkland Islands in 1970, is steadily being restored. In the meantime, visitors can walk around the interior, where the dining room is a reminder of former glory.

Along the waterfront

Also here is the **Maritime Heritage Museum** (same hours as *SS Great Britain*), detailing Bristol's history as a port and shipbuilding centre. The 20th century brought decline for the shipbuilding industry. By the 1920s there was only one commercial shipbuilding site left in Bristol, Stothert's Clifton Marine Engineering, and though their business picked up in World War II it was a steady decline to the launch of their last vessel, the *Miranda Guinness*, in 1976. A few years after this however, a new firm, David Abels, was formed, and is still operating today.

Inside the Industrial Museum

Return along the quay to the excellent ★ **Industrial Museum** (Tuesday to Sunday 10am–5pm, closed Monday, except Bank Holiday), a vast hangar-type structure with Bristol's shipping and aero-engine industries represented upstairs and the history of transport downstairs. Exhibits range from a cross-section of Concorde (produced in Bristol in 1969) to the accounts of an 18th-century slave ship.

This stretch of the quay offers good views of the cityscape. Behind Prince Street Bridge the 285-ft (87-m) spire of St Mary Redcliffe is clearly visible. To reach this historic church walk back to the bridge, cross Wapping Road and skirt Bathurst Basin.

St Mary Redcliffe

★★ **St Mary Redcliffe** was built between 1325–75 in the Perpendicular style, the last stage of English Gothic architecture in which verticals dominate, emphasised by pinnacles and projecting buttresses. Interesting features include the hexagonal 13th-century north porch with an inner 12th-century porch, elaborate fan vaulting (signature of the Perpendicular style), aisled transepts and a wealth of interesting memorials and effigies. Famous people associated with the church are the poets Thomas Chatterton (1752–70), who lived nearby, and Southey

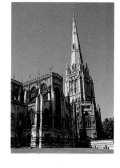

and Coleridge who were married to two sisters by the name of Fricker here in 1795.

Back at the docks, at the bottom of Redcliffe Hill, is *The Matthew*, a reconstruction of the ship in which John Cabot set sail for America in 1497 under patent of Henry VII.

Further sights

Also worth seeing is ★ **Wesley's New Room** (36 Horse-fair; 10am–1pm and 2–4pm), the oldest Methodist building in the world, founded by John Wesley in 1739, and now an engaging museum to Wesley and the Methodist movement. It lies in the centre of the old medieval city, near Broadmead shopping centre.

To take in ★★ **Dyrham Park** (National Trust; house:1 March to 29 October noon–5.30pm, closed Thursday and Friday, grounds: year-round daily noon–5.30pm; 12 miles/19km from Bristol) leave Bristol by the A420, turning left at the junction with the A46. The house is then signposted off to the left a few miles further on, not far from Hinton Hill, site of the Battle of Dyrham in 577, in which the Saxons gained control of Gloucester, Cirencester and Bath. Though built on the bones of a Tudor manor, the house you see today dates from 1692–1704 when William Blathwayt, Secretary of State to William III, re-modelled it in a loosely baroque style.

Dyrham Park

There have been few changes to the house since then, but the grounds were altered substantially around 1800 when improvements in the Bath-Gloucester road made an east entrance to the house more convenient than the existing west one. The formal gardens were moved to the east and the steeply rising hills, previously covered in terraces and walks, were turned into parkland. The work was carried out by Charles Harcourt-Masters (builder of the Holburne Museum in Bath, *see page 30*) with input from landscape architect Humphrey Repton. Only the staircase cascade of 224 steps in the spur of the hills (now dry and gathering weeds) remains of the previous design. The deer park, however, has existed here for centuries (*deor hamm* being Anglo-Saxon for deer enclosure).

Inside, the house incorporates a variety of Dutch and Flemish features (furniture, Delftware, paintings and engravings by Dutch artists, Flemish tapestries) reflecting William Blathwayt's diplomatic connections with Holland and his fluency in Dutch. **The Great Hall** (the only room retained from the Tudor manor) leads through the West Hall to the west terrace and gardens, from where, on the north side, a gate leads to the medieval parish church, filled with monuments to the Blathwayt family.

From Dyrham the A46 winds down Swainswick hill to Bath (8 miles/13km).

Excursion 3

The Mendip Hills

Prior Park – Chew Valley Lake – Cheddar Gorge *See map, p34–5*

This tour heads southwest of Bath to Cheddar Gorge in the Mendip Hills, one of southern England's most famous beauty spots and home of its most popular cheese. Though turned into a rather gaudy shrine to West Country pastoralism, Cheddar offers lovely walks and has lots of attractions for children. If you have time, and feel inclined to mix the vulgar and the sublime, this route links up well with Excursion 4 to Wells with its magnificent cathedral.

From Bath take the A36 Lower Bristol Road, passing on the left, after crossing the Kennet and Avon Canal, Prior Park Road (A3062) leading to the former village of Widcombe and **Prior Park**, the country home of Ralph Allen *(see page 8)*, built by John Wood the Elder between 1734 and 1742 close to Allen's stone quarries at Combe Down. With its imposing portico of towering Corinthian columns Prior Park is rated as one of the finest Palladian mansions in Britain. It was here that Allen held open house to the leading statesmen, writers and artists of the day, such as William Pitt, Alexander Pope, Henry Fielding and Gainsborough (the munificent Squire Allworthy in Fielding's *Tom Jones* is based on Allen). The building is now a school, but the ★ grounds have been taken over by the National Trust and are open to the public. The Palladian bridge spanning the fish ponds was built in around 1755.

Chew Valley Lake

The Lower Bristol Road is an industrial exit from Bath, running parallel with the railway line before joining the A4. Around 3 miles (5km) from Bath, take the A39 Wells road, then at Marksbury take the A368. At 15 miles (24km) from Bath, the road crosses the southern tip of ★ **Chew Valley Lake**, a reservoir created in 1956 which draws fly fishermen, sailors and birdlife. It has one of the largest reed beds in southwest England, inhabited by over 260 species of birds, including shovelers, gadwell, teal and the great crested grebe, and is skirted by meadows and woodland rich in butterflies, dragonflies and flora. Special trails (the Bittern Trail, the Grebe Trail), punctuated by hides, lead around the eastern shores of the lake. For details on fishing at Chew (and neighbouring Blagdon), *see page 71*.

Follow the A368 through West Harptree and then follow signposts to join the B3371 to Cheddar (25 miles/40km from Bath), passing en route the turning for Charterhouse, a centre for Roman lead mining and source of the lead sheets lining the Great Bath at Bath.

★★ **Cheddar Gorge**, the biggest gorge (3 miles/5km long) in Britain, was carved out of the karst limestone by the Yeo River. Much of it belongs the Marquess of Bath's **Cheddar Gorge and Showcaves**, though the north side is in the hands of the National Trust, and public footpaths crisscross the whole of the gorge. A range of entertainments have sprung up for tourists, who have been coming in droves to Cheddar ever since the railway to Bristol was opened in 1869. The chief attractions are the caves, which are the most spectacular in the warren of caves and swallowholes burrowing through the limestone Mendip Hills. ★ **Gough's Caves** (Easter to September 10am–5.30pm, October to Easter 10.30am–4.30pm, closed Christmas Eve and Christmas Day), carved out by the meltwaters of the last Ice Age and inhabited from the Stone Age, were discovered by Richard Gough in 1890 and opened to the public in 1898. It was here that the skeleton of the 9,000-year-old Cheddar Man was discovered in 1903. A walkway leads through a series of chambers encrusted with stalactites, whose colours range through grey (lead), red (iron oxide), green (copper carbonate) and white (calcium). The formations grow at the rate of approximately one cubic inch every thousand years.

Cheddar Gorge

Gough's Caves

The higher rate of admission to Gough's Cave also includes entrance to ★ **Cox's Cave** (discovered 1836), where the Crystal Quest presents a subterranean battle between good and evil, in which princesses and wizards prevail and dragons and goblins are defeated. Children love it, and even adults emerge smiling. Cox's Cave exits at **Jacob's Ladder**, a flight of 237 steps, each representing 1 million years in the life of the Earth (the history of man is equivalent to a piece of writing paper placed on the top step). Above the gorge, **Pavey's Tower** offers views over the Mendip Hills and beyond. A pretty walk leads for 5 miles (8km) around the top of the gorge.

Further down Cliff Road, the main street of Cheddar is packed with tea-rooms, glass-blowers, fudge-makers, cider barns and cheese shops. All of these come under one roof at **The Cheddar Gorge Cheese Co** (mid-March to 30 April daily 10am–4pm, 1 May to 30 September daily 10am–6pm) whose working dairy documents the history of cheese-making, which has been carried on in Cheddar for over 700 years. The dairy is augmented by a cooperage, spinner and potter. There are opportunities to sample products and, of course, to buy.

Cheddar Gorge Cheese Co

From Cheddar the A371 leads west to Axbridge, with the National Trust's **King John's Hunting Lodge**, a late medieval merchant's house (open 2–5pm). In the other direction, the A371 leads east along the edge of the Mendip Hills to Wells (11 miles/17km) (*see Excursion 4*).

Excursion 4

To Wells

Bath – Wells – Wookey Hole Caves – Glastonbury – Shepton Mallet *See map, p34–5*

In spite of the many stately homes, areas of outstanding natural beauty and tourist attractions surrounding Bath, for many people Wells Cathedral is the one compelling reason for venturing out of the city.

Priston Mill

The A367 road is clearly signposted from the south of Bath (like Excursion 3, it passes the road to Prior Park, *see page 44*). Eight miles (5km) from Bath a lane on the left leads to **Priston Mill** (Good Friday to 24 September 11am–5.30pm, school holidays Tuesday to Saturday 2.15–5pm), a working watermill used for grinding flour since 931, when it was given to the monks of Bath Abbey. At 17 miles (27km) from Bath the rural theme continues at the Chewton Cheese Dairy in Chewton Mendip where you can watch cheese being made every Thursday and Sunday.

As the road descends into Wells, a side road on the right leads for 2 miles (3km) to ★**Wookey Hole Caves** (summer daily 9.30am–5.30pm and winter daily 10.30am–4.30pm, closed 17 to 25 December) where guided tours explore caves carved out by the River Axe, which rises to the surface inside the caves. In competition with Cheddar, Wookey Hole offers other entertainments, mainly aimed at children, including an Edwardian fairground, a mirror maze and tours of the 19th-century paper mill.

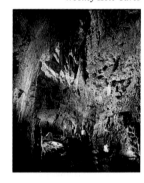

Wookey Hole Caves

46

Wells (population: 9,000), 23 miles (37km) from Bath, is a sleepy market town lifted completely out of the ordinary by its stunning ★★★ **Cathedral Church of St Andrew** and **Bishop's Palace**. Like Bath, it derives its name from natural springs which were probably associated with a pre-Christian shrine. In 705 a church was founded by Aldhelm, Bishop of Sherborne. The Diocese of Wells was created in 909, though the see was moved to Bath by John of Tours in around 1088. It returned to Wells under Bishop Savaric (1192), but in 1244 was split between the two cities with the creation of the Diocese of Bath and Wells.

The Cathedral that you see today was begun in 1179 and completed in 1340. It is in the Early English Gothic style, characterised by pointed arches and ribbed vaulting. Unlike Bath Abbey, it was a secular cathedral rather than a monastery and survived the Dissolution intact, though suffered repeated damage during the Civil War and Monmouth's Rebellion in the 17th century.

Market day in Wells

Parking is available either in the market place, from where the **Penniless Porch** – still used by beggars today – leads to the intricately carved **West Front** incorporating 293 statues of angels, kings, knights, bishops and saints (13th century) rising to a central band of 12 apostles (15th century) and the figure of Christ in Majesty at its apex, carved in 1985 by David Wynne to replace the crumbling original. Erosion and destruction by puritans in the 17th century have left many of the lower niches vacant, but the front remains a breathtaking sight, its unusual breadth due to the towers being placed either side of the nave instead of head on. Originally the statues would have numbered around 400 and been richly painted in bright colours.

Inside the cathedral, the eye is swept along the nave to the great scissor-arches at the transept, pulled by the succession of arches and the vaulted ceiling, whose delicate decoration was discovered under whitewash in the 19th century. In the Middle Ages the only seating in the cathedral would have been stone benches running around the sides of the naves and their aisles.

Pinnacle of the West Front

An anti-clockwise walk around the cathedral:

A   **Sugar Chantry** (1489). Commemorates Hugh Sugar, the cathedral's treasurer. Chantries were built by rich members of the congregation so that masses might be offered in memory of them after their death.

B   **The Font**. The base was brought from the old Saxon cathedral (on the site of the cloisters); the exquisite 17th-century cover was painted and gilded in 1982. Carvings on the pillars near the font depict scenes from everyday life in the Middle Ages: a man taking a thorn out of his foot, a cobbler at work, a man nursing a toothache. The scenes decorating one pillar, carved in around 1190, tells the complete story

Wells Cathedral

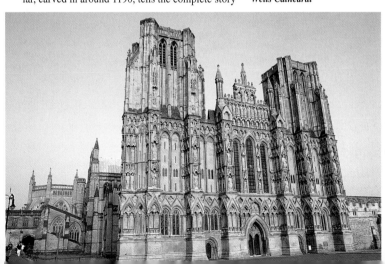

Choir and Jesse window

of a man and a boy stealing fruit from an orchard and being caught, chased and punished by the farmer.

C   Memorial Chapel to St Calixtus

D   Memorial Chapel to St Martin

E   ★★★ The Choir. This is the heart of the cathedral. On the underside of the seats are finely carved misericords (to support the clerics during periods in the service when they are required to stand). The east window (1340) depicts the lineage of Christ, with Jesse, King David (son of Jesse) and Mary. It is one of the oldest Jesse windows in Britain. High up above the choir are small niches where boy sopranos would have played the part of angels on feast days.

F   South Choir Aisle. A number of important tombs are found here: on the left (moving east), the Tomb of Bishop Harewell (1380), with its rebus (visual pun) on his name in the carving; the effigies of three Saxon Bishops, whose bones were transferred here from the Saxon cathedral in around 1200, when Wells was trying to regain cathedral status for the church of St Andrew; and the good Bishop Bekynton's tomb, with its grim reminder of death (the bishop's corpse rotting in his shroud) on the bottom rung. Beckington, Bishop of Bath and Wells between 1443–65 built the choir school over the West Cloister, the Chain Bridge and, for the people of Wells, a row of 12 houses in the marketplace. At the eastern end of the aisle are three examples of carved misericords (*see* E).

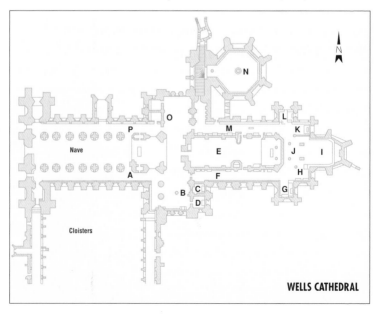

WELLS CATHEDRAL

G **St Catherine's Chapel**. The stained glass here was salvaged from a church in Rouen (desecrated during the French Revolution) in 1813.

H **St John the Baptist Chapel**

I ★★ **Lady Chapel**. Built in 1326, originally as a separate building. The Lady Chapel windows were shattered during the Civil War (1642–7) and Monmouth's Protestant Rebellion (1685). Only the upper sections contain the original glass. The brass lectern at the entrance to the Lady Chapel was given by Dean Robert Creyghton to mark the restoration of King Charles II in 1660.

J **Retrochoir**. Built to unite the Lady Chapel with the presbytery. The ribs in the lovely vaulting were decorated by T H Willement in 1845. Notice the magnificent 13th-century cope (cloak) chest nearby.

K **St Stephen's Chapel**

L **Chapel of Corpus Christi**. Reserved for private prayer.

M **North Choir Aisle**. Among the tombs are that of Bishop Giso (d.1088), brought here from the Saxon cathedral, and the alabaster tomb of Bishop Ralph of Shrewsbury (d. 1363), who founded the College of Vicars and built the Vicars' Hall.

49

Stairs to and ceiling of the Chapter House

N ★★★ **The Chapter House**. The curving flight of steps leading up to the octagonal Chapter House was built in the 13th century. Worn by age and wear, the lovely honey-coloured stone is illuminated by windows containing the oldest stained glass in the cathedral. The Chapter House itself, where cathedral business was carried out (and still is today on important occasions), was completed in 1306. Seating for 49 canons line the walls, each space marked by the name of the estate; above, 32 tiercorn ribs (precursor of fan vaulting) spray from a central pier. As you leave the Chapter House, a narrow flight of stairs (added in 1459) leads off to the Chain Bridge which links the cathedral with the Vicar's Hall.

O ★★★ **Clock**. This medieval clock is one of the treasures of the cathedral. It actually has two faces: one on the exterior wall of the cathedral, the other here. Still keeping time today (though the original internal mechanism is in the Science Museum in London) it comprises three dials, the outer one indicating the hours on a 24-hour clockface, the middle one showing the minutes, and the inner one marking the date of the lunar month. Try to catch the clock striking the hour, when jousting knights rotate.

This is also the best place to view the voluptuous ★★★ **scissor arches**, added by master mason William Joy between 1338–48. Though built to solve tech-

Scissor arches

nical problems – the weight of the tower, enlarged by Dean John Godelee in 1313, was straining the foundations – the visual effect is stunning.

P **Bubwith's Chantry**. In honour of Bishop Bubwith.

Cloister restaurant

The **Cloisters**, partly occupied by the cathedral shop and restaurant, are approached from the southwest side of the nave. Replacing the smaller 13th-century cloisters, they were completed in 1508. Above the East Cloister is the medieval library, financed by a legacy of Bishop Bubwith (d.1424), containing around 6,000 books. A door in the south cloister leads to the Bishop's Palace (also accessible from Market Place).

Bishop's Palace

The ★★ **Bishop's Palace** (Easter Saturday to 31 October, Tuesday, Wednesday, Thursday, Bank Holiday Mondays and throughout August 10am–6pm, Sunday 2–6pm) was begun in the early 13th century by Bishop Jocelin and enlarged by successive bishops until the mid-15th century. Moated and approached over a drawbridge, it was clearly designed for defence. Such features were added by Bishop Ralph of Shrewsbury in the 14th century.

The **Henderson Rooms** form the oldest part of the palace. In the First Floor Hall style, they comprise a ground-floor cellar from which a Jacobean staircase installed by Bishop Montague (1608–16) leads to a suite of state rooms: the **Long Gallery**, lined with portraits of past bishops, many of whom played key roles in English history; a Victorian-style **Drawing Room**, overlooking Bishop Jocelin's deer park (now pasture); the **Conference Room**, with its elaborate plaster ceiling and carpet from Windsor Castle; and **Panelled Room**, in which portraits of more recent bishops are displayed. Also open to visitors is the adjoining **Bishop's Chapel**, the private chapel of the Bishops of Bath and Wells.

In the tranquil grounds of the palace are the springs which gave Wells its name. They were harnessed by Bishop Beckynton in the 15th century to supply the palace with water and to drive the town's woollen mills. As you

Great Hall ruins

make your way back to the gatehouse, note the ruins of the **Great Hall**, built by Bishop Robert Burnell (1275–93). During the Reformation, the hall was the scene of the trial of the abbot and treasurer of Glastonbury Abbey, accused of sedition for their opposition to Henry VIII's severance from the Church of Rome. Found guilty, they were executed on Glastonbury Tor (*see page 51*).

From the gatehouse, a pleasant walk off to the left skirts the grounds of the palace, returning along St Andrew Street on the north side of the cathedral and passing ★★ **Vicar's Close**. This charming cobbled close was built in 1348 by Bishop Ralph of Shrewsbury to house 'Members of the

College of Vicars', clerics chosen for their singing voices. Over the gate is Vicar's Hall, where members dined, and at the far end of the street the chapel. Vicar's Hall is joined to the cathedral by the **Chain Bridge**.

Walking past the north side of the cathedral into Cathedral Green be sure to notice the exterior side of the clock, on which two medieval warriors mark time.

Glastonbury

From Wells, the A39 leads on to **Glastonbury** (population 6,800), the scene of an annual rock festival and the oldest Christian foundation in Britain. The ★★ **ruined abbey** is built on the site of a much earlier church, according to legend dating from the 1st century, when Joseph of Arimethea is supposed to have brought either the Holy Grail or the Blood of the Cross here. St Patrick and St Bridget visited the abbey in the 5th century, and Edmund I (d. 946), Edgar (d. 975) and Edmund Ironside (d.1016) are all buried here. The buildings that you see date from between 1184 and 1303, when Glastonbury was the richest Benedictine abbey in England, bar Westminster: they fell into ruins after the Dissolution. Remains of a warrior and his female companion, interred in front of the high altar, are identified as King Arthur and Queen Guinevere by local legend. Winter flowering hawthorns in the abbey's grounds are supposed to have sprung from the Holy Thorn borne here by the staff of Joseph (*see above*). **Glastonbury Tor**, above the town, offers views as far as the Bristol Channel. It was here that the last abbot, Richard Whiting, and abbey treasurer, John Arthur Thorne, were executed in 1539 for opposing Henry VIII.

Just south of Glastonbury is **Street**, site of Millfield public school and the headquarters of the shoe company Clark's, founded in 1825 by wool dealer and rug-maker Cyrus Clark, who was soon running a profitable business making wool-lined slippers. Clarke's Village (a factory-price outlet for well-known brands, ranging from Royal Brierley to Jaeger, Crabtree & Evelyn and even Thorntons chocolates) includes a shoe museum.

A return to Bath along the picturesque A361 to **Shepton Mallet** (9 miles/5km from Glastonbury) passes the **Pilton Manor vineyards** (opportunities to buy local wine) and, 3 miles (5km) east of Shepton Mallet, Cranmore, departure point for the **East Somerset Steam Railway** (tel: 01749 880417 for timetable). From Shepton Mallet, the A 37 passes Downside abbey and school (established by Benedictine monks in 1814) to pick up the A367 to Bath via Radstock, where **Radstock, Midsomer Norton & District Museum** (Saturday 10am–4pm, Sunday and Bank Holidays 2–5pm) recalls 19th-century life in a north Somerset coalfield. The last coal was mined here in 1973.

The ruined abbey

51

East Somerset Steam Railway

Stonehenge

Excursion 5

To Longleat and Stonehenge

Longleat – Warminster – Stonehenge – Stourhead *See map, p34–5*

Longleat (22 miles/35 km from Bath), home of the Marquess of Bath, is one of the southwest's top tourist attractions, as is Stonehenge, located a further 14 miles (22 km) to the southeast. A full day is required for Longleat alone, especially if you want to see both the Safari Park, and during school holidays early arrival is advised.

Leave Bath along the A36 via Claverton Manor (see Route 5). After 10 miles (16km), the road passes the **Tropical Bird Gardens at Rode** (summer daily 10am–6.30pm, winter 10am–dusk), where tropical and rare birds inhabit 17 acres/6.9 hectares of woodland and garden.

★★ **Longleat** (house: Easter to 30 September 10am–6pm, rest of the year 10am–4pm, closed Christmas Day; safari park: 11 March to 29 October 10am–6pm, last admission 5.30pm or sunset) is signposted from the roundabout at Beckington. There are a range of admission charges, depending on which attractions you want to visit. A 'passport ticket' grants access to all of them. Completely separate from the house and safari park, but occupying 400 acres of Longleat Forest (off the A36) is **Center Parcs**, a family-oriented country-club-cum-theme-park where the theme is the great outdoors. This was introduced by the 7th Marquess in 1994.

Henry Thynne, the 6th Marquess of Bath, opened Longleat to the public in 1949, a course of action partly necessitated by heavy death duties following the death of the 5th Marquess in 1946. It was the first stately home to go public, but others soon followed suit. Since then Longleat has spawned into a huge entertainment complex attracting some 500,000 tourists a year. As well as the safari park (opened in 1966) there are safari boats to 'gorilla island' on the Half Mile Lake, a butterfly garden, a miniature railway, a Dr Who exhibition, a flight simulator, vintage cars, the 'world's largest maze' and Postman Pat Village, a huge ragbag of attractions which threaten to eclipse the house itself. The abiding pleasure of Longleat, however, is the vast parkland, which dispels the sense of tawdriness felt elsewhere. Visitors can roam more or less as they please and fish in the lower reaches of the lake.

The wealthy Thynne family have modest roots. The founder of the dynasty, John Thynne (1515–80), began his working life as a clerk in the kitchen of the Tudor court. His prospects rocketed when, under the patronage of the

Longleat's miniature railway and the world's largest maze

Protector of Somerset, he was made a knight of the realm for services in battle against the Scots at Pinkie in 1547. With knighthood came prestige and wealth, and between 1559–80 he built Longleat. His grandson, Thomas Thynne, introduced royal blood to the line through his second marriage to Catherine Lyte Howard, descendant of the 1st Duke of Norfolk whose ancestors included Edward I and Alfred the Great. In 1682, Thomas's grandson was made the 1st Viscount Weymouth, and in 1789 the 3rd Viscount Weymouth was made 1st Marquess of Bath by George III.

Longleat House

The first room you come to on entering the ★★ **house** and turning right from the reception is the ★★ **Great Hall**, a vast panelled room 35ft (10.6m) high, complete with minstrels' gallery, which is the one room predominantly dating from the Elizabethan era. Exhibits include the blood-stained tunic worn by Charles I on his execution. Leading on from here are a series of extravagantly ornate rooms, whose impeccable upkeep (fresh flowers, polished wood and gleaming silver) creates a comfortable, lived-in quality in spite of the opulence (much of which was created in the Italian style by the designer J. D. Crace for the Fourth Marquess of Bath): the Lower East Corridor (fine Flemish tapestries from the 17th century), the Italian-style Ante Library and Red Library (containing some of Longleat's 40,000 books), Breakfast Room, Lower Dining Room (with Crace ceiling adapted from the Doge's Palace in Venice) and the sumptuous state rooms (dining room, saloon, drawing room and suite of state bedrooms). It was from the State Drawing Room that Titian's *Rest on the Flight to Egypt* was stolen in 1995.

53

Also open to the public (by appointment) are some of the corridors and halls covered in 3-D murals (paint mixed with sawdust) by the current Marquess, whose notoriously unconventional lifestyle frequently delights British tabloids. Begun in the 1960s these murals now cover around a third of the house.

Among the attractions that occupy the outbuildings is *The Life and Times of Lord Bath*, an exhibition dedicated to the Sixth Marquess with special emphasis on World War II. As well as Churchilliana there is a collection of watercolours by Adolf Hitler, whom the Sixth Marquess admitted to admiring.

One of the 'Lions of Longleat'

The ★ **Safari Park** is a 15-minute drive from the house. It comprises a series of parkland enclosures in which, except where the animals are deemed fairly harmless (giraffes, zebra, antelopes, etc) you are required to stay in your vehicle with the windows closed (or take one of the special buses). The lions remain the stars of the show, though the monkeys display comic talent by making off with windscreen wipers and other detachables.

From Longleat, the A36 leads south to Warminster (population: 15,000) and then, 17 miles (27km) further on, Salisbury Plain, on which looms Britain's most evocative ancient monument, ★★★ **Stonehenge** (1 April to 30 September 10am–6pm, 1 October to 31 March 10am–4pm), a UNESCO World Heritage site. Spanning the period 3,000–1,000 BC (the central ring of stones dates from around 2,000BC), it comprises two types of stones, 123 bluestones, hauled here from the Preseli mountains in Pembrokeshire, 200 miles (320km), and the larger sarsen stones which outcrop locally. Its purpose has baffled archaeologists and other experts for centuries and engendered many myths. Inigo Jones, one of the first to investigate its purpose, at the behest of James I, concluded it was a Roman temple to Uranus. Though the alignment of the major axis with the midsummer sunrise suggests a religious purpose, no firm evidence has been found, and theories range from the practical – a calendar – to the extraterrestrial.

Stourhead's grounds

In the other direction, along the B3092, 3 miles (5km) north of Mere, is the village of Stourton and ★★ **Stourhead** (house: 1 April to 31 October noon–5.30pm or dusk, closed Thursday and Friday; garden: all year daily 9–7pm or sunset), a Palladian mansion built in 1721–24 by Colen Campbell, whose grounds represent one of the finest expressions of the early 18th-century landscape movement. A satisfying arrangement of formal gardens, dells, knolls, lake and parkland enfold temples to Flora and Apollo, picturesque bridges, a cascade, a Gothic cottage, a grotto and the parish church, creating a delightful theatre for the drama of the changing seasons. Horace Walpole thought the gardens here 'one of the most picturesque scenes in the world'. On the west side of the garden a footpath leads to **Alfred's Tower**, an 18th-century brick folly on the borders of Wiltshire, Somerset and Dorset.

Excursion 6

The Road to London

Corsham Court – Lacock Abbey – Sheldon Manor – Bowood House – Avebury Stone Circles *See map, p34–5*

Though designed as an excursion from Bath, the tour described here works just as well in reverse as part of a leisurely day's drive from London (take the M4 as far as Chieveley (junction 13), then the A4 through Newbury, Hungerford and Marlborough.

The A4 was the main route to London not just before the M4 was built, but for centuries. It links a series of old English towns important to the medieval cloth trade (as was Bath) and it was along here that the London stage coach brought many of the city's 18th-century visitors. In 1667 it took three days for a coach to make the journey from London to Bath, but by 1711 the time had been cut to between 30 and 38 hours, providing highwaymen were kept at bay and heavy luggage was taken separately. Reflecting its historical importance, the road has a number of grand 18th-century estates within easy striking distance, and these form the core of this tour.

Leaving Bath via Bathampton (a pretty village also accessible by boat from Bath Boating Station, *see page 71*) the road climbs to Box.

Off to the right, some 15km (9 miles) from Bath, is ★★ **Corsham Court** (Good Friday to 30 September 2–6.30pm, closed Monday; rest of the year except December 2–4.30pm closed Monday and Friday; closed December) whose delightful informality – characterful retainers, peacocks mooching in the hallway, the master's dogs seeking titbits – was captured in a cameo documentary by the BBC shortly before the death of the Sixth Lord Methuen in 1995.

The current building dates from 1582, when it was built on or near the site of an ancient manor house that had served as a country retreat for Saxon kings. It came into the hands of the Methuen family, who still owns it, in 1745, after which its north (rear) side gained a Palladian facade (later replaced). In around 1760 it was enlarged by Capability Brown, who duplicated the wings on the south front and converted the east wing into a suite of state rooms (open to the public today). Further changes were made in 1800 when John Nash replaced the Palladian-style north front with a building in the style of Strawberry Hill Gothic, but this was substantially changed again in the 1840s by the architect Thomas Bellamy, in an attempt to rid the house of damp.

Corsham Court

The chief treasures of Corsham are its paintings, many of them acquired by Sir Paul Methuen (1672–1757), the godfather of the Methuen who bought Corsham. All the rooms contain fine works of art, but most richly endowed is the **Picture Gallery**, specially designed by Capability Brown to house Sir Paul's collection and hung with red silk damask. Highlights here include Van Dyck's *Betrayal of Christ* and *A Man in a Ruff*, works by Bernardo Strozzi and Borgognone, and Sofonisba Anguisciola's attractive *Three Gaddi Children*. Complementing the paintings is furniture by Chippendale and the Adam brothers, whose handiwork also graces the other rooms. More paintings are found in the **Cabinet Room**, including an exquisite Annunciation from the studio of Fra Filippo Lippi and the *Flying Cherub*, a cartoon by Cesari for a mosaic in the cupola of St Peter's in Rome; and the **State Bedroom**, containing a portrait of Pope Gregory XV by Reni. The **Octagon Room** includes *The Sleeping Cupid* (1496), attributed (dubiously) to Michelangelo in the catalogue, and an allegorical portrait by an unknown artist of a troubled Elizabeth I flanked by death and having her crown removed by two cherubs, which is supposed to refer to her feelings of remorse following the execution of her former favourite, Robert Devereux, Earl of Essex.

Outside, gravel walks lead to a **Bath House**, designed by Capability Brown, with its 15th-century **Bradford Porch**, taken from a house called The Priory in Bradford-on-Avon (*see page* 38), where the Methuen family's wool business was based. Also in the village of Corsham (in Park Lane) is the **Underground Quarry** (April and October, Sunday only; May to September daily except Friday; closed in winter) where guided tours of the shaft stone mine trace the history of mining the creamy Bath stone.

A few miles further along the A4 (14miles/22km from Bath), the A350 leads off to Lacock Abbey in the delightfully unspoilt village of **Lacock**. Lacock's immediate appeal lies not only in its quaint architecture, but in its lack, thanks to the National Trust which owns the village, of telegraph wires, poles and road markings. For this reason it has been a location in a number of films and television costume dramas, and served as Meryton in the BBC's 1995 production of *Pride and Prejudice*.

★★ **Lacock Abbey**, an intriguing mix of medieval, Renaissance and Gothic architecture, was founded in 1232 by Ela Countess of Salisbury as a nunnery for Augustinian canonesses. Following the Dissolution of the Monasteries in 1539 Henry VIII pensioned off the nuns and sold the property to William Sharrington, who set about converting it into a home. Sharrington's conversion retained many of the original features of the 13th-

House in Corsham

Lacock Abbey entrance and cloisters

century abbey, including the buildings flanking the cloister court. He partitioned the nuns' refectory and dormitories to create the Brown Gallery and Stone Gallery and added the octagonal tower and swizzlestick chimney stacks. Much of the fine masonry of this period is attributed to John Chapman, mason to Henry VIII.

Cloister window

Later, in the mid-18th century, John Ivory Talbot commissioned Sanderson Miller, the architect who inspired the rage for sham ruins and follies, to make alterations in the Gothic style – pointed-arch windows, medieval style masonry – again in harmony with the building's ecclesiastical origins. The **Hall** was entirely remodelled, with ogee-arched niches containing terracotta statuettes and a ceiling covered in the coats of arms of Talbot's friends and neighbours. In the 19th century Talbot's great grandson, William Henry Fox Talbot, altered the south side, introducing the oriel windows. Fox Talbot had a keen interest in the sciences. As well as being a respected botanist, he made important contributions to the development of photography. In 1840 he discovered the calotype process, in which an image was produced on paper treated with silver iodide and developed by sodium thiosulphite. His negative of an oriel window in Lacock's South Gallery is the oldest in existence. The abbey's barn houses the **Fox Talbot Museum of Photography**.

The **Cloister** is flanked by 14th- and 15th-century rooms belonging to the original nunnery, including the Chaplain's Room (on the south walk) and the Sacristy, Chapter House and Warming Room (east walk). The stone coffins in the latter were found in the grounds.

The village of **Lacock** is enchanting. Standing out among its 13th-century stone and half-timbered cottages is the imposing red-brick Red Lion inn (good food, plus accommodation), next door to which is a tiny museum dedicated to packaging. Stand and surrender to the nostalgia conjured up by the labels of yesteryear, from Zebo black grate polish to favourite childhood confectionery.

On the north side of the A4, signposted off the A420 2½ miles (4km) from Chippenham, is **Sheldon Manor** (April 15 to 1 October Sunday, Thursday and Bank Holidays, house from 2pm, gardens 12.30pm), the only surviving building of a medieval village. Its chief architectural draw is its superb 13th-century porch. A little further afield (3 miles/5km) in this direction, off the B4039, is **Castle Combe**, the archetypal English village (here Cotswold in character), much visited by tourists but retaining most of its charm.

Sheldon Manor inside and out

Close to the village is the **Castle Combe Skid Pan and Kart Track** (tel: 01249 782101) where an open grand prix is held on the first Saturday of every month.

Bowood House and gardens

The last of the grand houses on this tour is ★★ **Bowood House** (1 April to 29 October daily 10am–6pm) 2½ miles (4km) off the A4, a few miles east of Chippenham. The Palladian home of the Earl and Countess of Shelburne, it offers a fine interior, including the laboratory where Dr Joseph Priestley discovered oxygen, extensive grounds and a well designed adventure playground for children. What you see today is only a part of the original house. The 'Big House', formerly adjoining the eastern end, was demolished in 1955.

Entrance is through the **orangery**, designed by Robert Adam in 1769. Adam was employed by the 1st Marquess of Lansdowne to complete an existing, unfinished house which his father had bought in 1754. Once filled with tubs of orange and lemon trees, this long, light gallery was used for special occasions. During a royal visit by King Edward VII and Queen Alexandria in 1907 it was decked out with palms and a Persian tent. A number of the cabinets are filled with mementoes relating to the 5th Lord of Lansdowne's term as Viceroy of India (1888–94), including letters from Queen Victoria.

Off the orangery (turn right as you enter the house) is the **laboratory** in which oxygen was discovered (1774) by Dr Joseph Priestley, the librarian and tutor to the two sons of the 1st Lord Lansdowne. Lansdowne, a flamboyant character who served as prime minister for a while (he was described by Disraeli as 'the ablest and most accomplished statesman of the 18th century') patronised the arts and sciences. Bowood's laboratory was later used by John Ingenhouse who discovered photosynthesis and helped develop inoculation against smallpox.

The **library** was designed by Robert Adam in 1769, but was substantially altered by the architect C. R. Cockerell in 1821–24, including the coffered ceiling. In the middle of the orangery two bronze doors lead to the private chapel, also remodelled by Cockerell, which is still used for special services today. Highlights in the exhibition rooms upstairs include the Albanian costume worn by Lord Byron and the **Lansdowne Napoleonic Collection** containing Napoleon's bronze death mask.

The **grounds** of Bowood are suitably grand, and especially delightful in spring when the rhododendrons and azaleas bloom (the rhododendron park is open during the flowering season between mid-May to the end of June). The long lake below the terraces was created by Capability Brown in the 1760s. Its north end features a Doric temple, cascade and 'hermit's cave', all added at a later date. A fine mausoleum, designed by Adam, stands in the rhododendron park.

Striking a pose in Bowood's grounds

From Calne (19 miles/30km from Bath) the A4 crosses the chalk Downs (notice **Lansdowne Column** and a 'white horse', one of several hereabouts which was carved in 1780 on the hill to the right), which together with Salisbury Plain forms one of the richest prehistoric landscapes in Europe. It is dotted with the dolmens and standing stones of Iron Age farmers. ★★ **Avebury Stone Circle**, 1 mile (2km) north of the A4 is the largest circle in Britain. Hauled here from Marlborough Downs, 3 miles (5km) away, some 4,000 years ago, the sarsen stones (extremely hard-wearing sandstone which scatters the downs and Salisbury Plain) form one large circle surrounded by a ditch (originally twice as deep as it is today) and two sets of smaller concentric circles (spanned by Avebury village which has grown up among the stones). The site was used for ceremonial purposes, a role revived by Druids and New Agers at the winter and summer solstices and spring and autumn equinoxes. A concrete post in the centre of an inner circle marks the spot of the Obelisk, a tall thin stone around which human bones have been found. Also of interest in the village is the 17th-century Great Barn holding a museum of rural life and Avebury Manor (National Trust), a late 16th-century building with Queen Anne alterations.

Back on the A4, a few miles further on, the road passes the mysterious **Silbury Hill** (on the left), the largest manmade mound in Europe (purpose unknown), and, signposted across fields to the right, **West Kennet Long Barrow Tomb**, 5,000 years old and one of the largest chambered tombs in Britain. Access is allowed into part of the tomb, where votive offerings to Pan are sometimes found – an ear of wheat, a daisy, a lighted candle.

This tour ends at the attractive market town of **Marlborough**, whose colonnaded high street offers a lively central market and a clutch of good tea-shops popular with pupils at the town's famous public school.

59

Among Avebury's ancient stones

Silbury Hill

Architecture

The Palladian style

The style of architecture exemplified by Bath is known as Palladian, after the late-Renaissance Venetian architect Andrea Palladio (1508–80), whose buildings and writings inspired the style. Palladio's own inspiration (Venice's Il Redentore and San Giorgio Maggiore churches and the Teatro Olimpico) was the architecture of ancient Greece and Rome, whose governing principles were symmetry and proportion, as laid down by Vetruvius, author of the only work on architecture to survive from Roman times. There were five styles of classical architecture (the Five Orders): Doric, Ionic, Corinthian, Tuscan and Composite (a mixture of Corinthian and Ionic), each represented by its pillars which dictated the proportions of the style as a whole. These proportions not only applied to the facade of a building, but also to its interior, where the position of skirting, dado and cornice all had to mirror the proportions of the classical column.

Palladianism was first introduced to Britain by Inigo Jones as early as 1620. It was revived a century later, around 1715, when Lord Burlington brought the Venetian architect Giacomo Leoni to England to work on a book of Palladio's designs. This book, along with a volume called *Vitruvius Britannicus* by the architect Colin Campbell, became a pattern book not only for architects but also for master builders.

61

The John Woods

The architect credited with introducing the Palladian style to Bath is John Wood the Elder (1704–54), who had worked with Palladian architects in London. Though individual Palladian buildings had already been erected in the city (for example, General Wolfe's House, at No 5 Trim Street), he conceived of whole streets and terraces in the Palladian style, something which Bath's urgent need for accommodation made viable. What's more, Bath's growing fashionableness among England's upper classes made a grandiose style of architecture appropriate.

Queen Square and the Royal Mineral Water Hospital

Wood was partly inspired by Bath's Roman heritage (even though most of Aquae Sulis was unexcavated at the time), envisaging a 'Royal Forum', a 'Grand Circus' and an 'Imperial Gymnasium'. In the end, side-tracked by other projects such as Prior Park (*see page 44*), he achieved only a small part of this dream: Queen Square (1729–39), the North and South parades (1740–43), the Royal Mineral Water Hospital (1742), and the Circus (1754–67), which his son, John Wood the Younger, finished.

John Wood the Younger embraced his father's vision totally. He transformed the Upper Town, then bordering

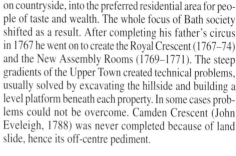

Royal Crescent

on countryside, into the preferred residential area for people of taste and wealth. The whole focus of Bath society shifted as a result. After completing his father's circus in 1767 he went on to create the Royal Crescent (1767–74) and the New Assembly Rooms (1769–1771). The steep gradients of the Upper Town created technical problems, usually solved by excavating the hillside and building a level platform beneath each property. In some cases problems could not be overcome. Camden Crescent (John Eveleigh, 1788) was never completed because of land slide, hence its off-centre pediment.

From Palladian to neoclassical and Gothic

The reason the Palladian style is so pervasive in Bath is due to several factors: the city's rapid expansion during the 18th century (coupled with the demolition of earlier buildings) and the way the dramatic contours of the city lent visual variety to the terraces and crescents thus saving the style from palling. Added to this was the ready availability of Bath stone following the opening of Ralph Allen's quarries on Combe Down. The soft limestone blocks can be easily shaped by the mason's chisel and together create a perfectly smooth facade which looks like a single piece of stone (though this was only deemed necessary for the front facade – the backs of Bath's buildings are often undressed rubble).

However, Palladianism wasn't totally static. Buildings from the first half of the century are different in many ways from those at the end. Decorative baroque details around doors and windows, popular until about 1730 (Wood's Queen Square), gave way to much plainer frames, and by the end of the 1760s there was virtually no detail at all. The Circus, with its decorative frieze and parapet, are in contrast to the plain Royal Crescent which derives its impact from its commanding position and great sweep of 114 Ionic columns. In addition, despite the great pains taken by the architects and builders to create seamless facades, householders still liked to put their own individual stamp on a building, perhaps with a more elaborate doorcase to reflect their greater prestige.

Corinthian columns (above) and Ionic columns (below)

But by the 1770s the tide was turning and Palladianism, with its clean straight lines, was developing into neoclassicism, a less rigorous interpretation of the classical style with finer decorative details and more graceful lines, exemplified by the architect and furniture-designer Robert Adam. It was partly prompted by architects going abroad on the Grand Tour and seeing the ruins of the Greek and Roman civilisations for themselves. Robert Adam had studied in Rome, but instead of directly copying what he had seen there, he used the motifs and ideas as a springboard for his imagination.

Heavily influenced by Adam was Thomas Baldwin (most of the development on the east side of Pulteney Bridge, the Guildhall, Bath Street and the Cross Bath. Compare John Wood the Younger's austere Hot Bath (1778) with Baldwin's nearby Cross Bath (1780s), with its sinuous curves and finely carved friezes. Other architects active in Bath at the time were John Palmer (Lansdown Crescent 1789–93, the Grand Pump Room) and John Eveleigh (Camden Crescent 1788, Somerset Place 1790).

Georgian window and the Guildhall

Meanwhile, from the mid-18th century Gothic elements occasionally crept in, adding a touch of romance. Ogee windows can sometimes be found in an otherwise classical facade. Bath's most notable example of Gothic is the Countess of Huntingdon's Chapel (1765), with its castellated parapet and ogee-arched windows. The Gothic style was especially appropriate to garden architecture and, which became increasingly popular as gardens grew larger and, in the country at least, incorporated parkland, lakes and streams. The ubiquitous temples, obelisks and 'pantheons' were often relieved by a Gothic feature or two, as at Stourhead *(see page 54)*. And Gothic ruins and follies were fashionable until well into the 19th century. In Bath, Ralph Allen hired Sanderson Miller to build the Gothic Sham Castle (1762) on Claverton Down, and Bath eccentric William Beckford had Lansdown Tower (1827), a 154-ft (53-m) high tower-cum-minaret, built on the top of Lansdown Hill.

63

The interiors

As a rule, Bath interiors are rather plain, even though Georgian houses in other cities are often quite lavish inside. Most housing was intended for short-stay guests, in town for the season, and landlords were loath to waste money on unnecessary ornament. The obvious exceptions are the great public buildings such as the Assembly Rooms and the Guildhall and fine houses specifically built for their occupants. In the case of the Assembly Rooms, the splendid interior is in marked contrast to the plain exterior: in the ballroom, decorated friezes, a plinth mounted by 12-ft (3.6-m) high Corinthian columns, and Vitruvian scrollwork; in the tea room Ionic and Corinthian columns, gilded iron railings, and coves decorated with carvings of foliage. Incidentally, these rooms are painted in colours (a warm yellow and dark peppermint) appropriate to the period. During the latter half of the century internal walls were plastered rather than panelled, making the delicate decorative details favoured by Adam easier to achieve. The Banqueting Hall of Baldwin's Guildhall, heavily influenced by Adam, is filled with exquisitely carved details. Following the birth of publications such as the monthly *Builder's Magazine* Adam's designs were widely imitated.

Guildhall interior

Victorian adjustments

The Georgian period came to an end in 1830. The Victorians, whose forte was industrial design, had less clearly defined ideas about architecture. Grand buildings were built in any one of several revivalist styles, with neoclassical jostling with Greek revival and Gothic. Ordinary housing for the growing middle and lower-middle classes was supplied by bay-windowed villas, which spread in ribbons south and west entwining many old villages.

The Victorians are blamed for spoiling many of the Georgian facades by building out (Adam's Pulteney Bridge, for example, acquired ugly extensions, still seen on the unrestored rear side). And whereas the Georgians had been careful to conceal drainpipes, either taking them down the back of buildings or hiding them in the front wall, the Victorians had fewer aesthetic scruples. Sometimes they painted the facades, by then black from pollution (painted advertisements became popular, *see page 30*), and often tampered with their proportions, extending the length of windows to let in more light and replacing the small panes of Georgian glass with sheet glass.

64

Victoria Art Gallery and the dome of the Pump Room's concert hall

But attempts were made to adapt some Georgian buildings sensitively. J. M. Brydon extended the Guildhall and added the Victoria Art Gallery. He also added the domed concert hall to the Pump Room and was responsible for incorporating the newly excavated Great Bath into the Pump Room and King's Bath ensemble. Similarly, great efforts were made to integrate the Kennet and Avon Canal (1810) and the Great Western Railway (1840). Both cut right through the city yet don't detract from its beauty.

Post World War II

In World War II Bath was hit by the Baedeker raids, a bombing campaign aimed at cities of outstanding cultural significance. A heavy programme of restoration ensued, in many cases taking decades to complete. Where the damage was beyond repair, and sometimes simply in the name of making the city more suited to 20th-century living, the old was swept away and replaced by modern blocks of shops and offices. Though in Bath stone (or artificial Bath stone), as dictated by the Bath Act of 1925, the new buildings were almost universally disliked, provoking a barrage of opposition to future redevelopments. Nowadays, Bath's planners must chart a difficult course between conservation and regeneration, resulting in some peculiar pseudo-classical hybrids such as the Podium, in Northgate Street. What's more, tastes change. What was deemed execrable and fit only for demolition a decade or two ago may suddenly be championed by new aesthetic values – which is exactly what has happened to the Empire Hotel, an Edwardian pile overlooking Parade Gardens.

The Arts

Bath has had a vigorous cultural life ever since Beau Nash introduced a small orchestra of six London-trained musicians in the early 1700s. Today, special festivals ensure it maintains an international reputation as a centre for the arts, but even on an everyday level the city lives and breathes music and performance art (nourished by tourism). Abbey Churchyard is a stage for fire-eaters, jugglers and clowns, while street musicians – from African drummers to string quartets – are encountered at every turn. On summer weekends music fills the city's parks.

Music: venues and festivals

Events are regularly held in the Assembly Rooms, the Pump Room, the Guildhall and the Abbey (for details, consult *This Month in Bath,* free from the Tourist Information Centre). Bath International Music Festival (mid-May to early June) is a two-week whirlwind of concerts held in venues throughout Bath. One of Britain's most important music festivals, it attracts classical and jazz performers from across the world. (Box office, tel: 01225 463362.)

Jazz performer and Bath Festival Concert

65

Bath Festivals Trust which runs the festival also organises the International Chamber Music series, a programme of six concerts which runs through the winter, again attracting international musicians. Later in the year, a Bach festival (October) and a Mozartfest (November; box office: as International Music Festival) are held. The run-up to Christmas offers seasonal concerts, including a performance of Handel's *Messiah* in Bath Abbey.

Literary events

The many authors who have lived in or visited Bath over the centuries are celebrated in the Book Museum (Monday to Friday 9am–1pm and 2–5.30pm, Saturday 9.30am–1pm) in Manvers Street. Evening literary tours (fun rather than scholarly), pinpointing who lived where and revealing the real-life inspiration for fictional places and events, are run by Litera tours at 7.30pm on Monday, Tuesday and Wednesday evenings in summer (contact the Rummer pub, tel: 01225 460332). Bath Literature Festival (February and March) includes readings, plays, talks and performances, with 50 percent of the programme aimed at children.

Theatre

The Theatre Royal has a varied programme, consistently featuring well-known actors and actresses. The box office is open Monday to Saturday 10am–8pm. Tours of the theatre are held on Wednesday and Saturday at 11am. Cabaret and comedy are celebrated at the Fringe Festival (held around the same time as the music festival).

Fringe Festival act

Food and Drink

Opposite:
The Sally Lunn bun

Bath has two claims to fame on the culinary front: the Bath bun, which is much in evidence in its tea-rooms, and the Bath Oliver biscuit, a white biscuit invented by Dr William Oliver in the 18th century to suit the delicate digestion of invalids and now, thanks to the entrepreneurial instincts of the doctor's coachman who inherited the secret recipe, the preferred companion to Stilton cheese. But there are several more recherché specialities to be discovered, including the Bath sausage (fresh pork, Wiltshire bacon, spinach and Dijon mustard), available from the **Sausage Shop** (7 Green Street) and traditional local cheeses such as Tornegus (a soft Caerphilly-type cheese with a rind washed in wine and herbs), sold by cheesemonger **Paxton & Whitfields** (1 John Street). Lastly, there is **Sally Lunn's** bun (enormous though surprisingly light and digestible) invented by Bath baker Sally Lunn in around 1680. Infinitely versatile, the Lunn bun comes in many different guises – from a raft for Welsh rarebit or chicken curry to a fluffy underpinning for strawberry jam and clotted cream.

South of Bath, there is no escaping West Country specialities such as cider and Cheddar cheese, which have become an integral part of the region's tourist industry. In Bath, however, sophistication rather than rusticity is the order of the day, for in keeping with the city's long tradition of providing pleasures the city is well endowed with restaurants. They range from the esteemed Hole in the Wall offering the best in 'modern British cooking' to the spicily fragrant Mai-Thai. Wherever you dine, be sure to book, especially in summer and on weekends.

67

Restaurants

£££ expensive (over £50 for two); **££** moderate (£30-50 for two); **£** inexpensive (under £30 for two). Price brackets include house wine.

The Hole in the Wall

The Hole in the Wall, 16 George Street, tel: 01225 425242. A long-established restaurant which has been revived to great acclaim. Highly imaginative haute cuisine. **£££**

The Olive Tree

The Olive Tree, Queensberry Hotel, Russel Street, tel: 01225 447928. 'Foodie' favourite, serving modern British cooking, with French, Italian and Moroccan influences. Situated below the Queensberry Hotel. **£££**

The Royal Crescent Hotel, Royal Crescent, tel: 01225 739955. Within the walled gardens of the hotel. Fine food, elegant surroundings. **£££**

Clos du Roy, 1 Seven Dials Close, tel: 01225 444450. Fancy food, stylish setting, jazz pianist. **£££**

The Moon and Sixpence

The Moon and Sixpence, 6a Broad Street, tel: 01225 460962. Modern British food, plus some foreign imports. Old favourites are given an imaginative twist. Attractive setting. Recommended. **££**

The New Moon, Seven Dials, tel: 01225 444407. All-day brasserie convenient for the theatre. Offshoot of the older Moon and Sixpence. **££**

Claret's, Kingsmead Square, tel: 01225 466688. Mainly French, plus modern British. Light options – such as pancakes – also available. Al fresco dining in summer. **££**

Mai Thai, 6 Pierrepont Street, tel: 01225 445557. Excellent Thai in Georgian setting. **££**

Sally Lunn's, 4 North Parade Passage, tel: 01225 461634. An excellent option for a lunchtime snack, but poor value during the evening, when the tea-room converts to a candlelit restaurant. **£** at lunchtime, **££** in the evening.

Rajpoot, Argyle Street, tel: 01225 466833. First-rate cooking from Rajasthan. **££**

Just Duck Szechuan, The Podium, Northgate Street, tel: 01225 481333. Crispy Szechuan duck a speciality, but large range of other dishes too. **££**

68

Footlights, The Podium, Northgate Street, tel: 01225 480366. Tex-Mex restaurant in conservatory setting. **£–££**

Demuth's, 2 North Parade, tel: 01225 446059. Good vegetarian restaurant open all day. Licensed. **£**

P.J. Peppers

P. J. Peppers, 5 Edgar Buildings, George St Bath, tel: 01225 465777. Lively café-bar open for breakfast and closing around 9pm. Good for an early evening drink and light snack. **£**

Pizza Express, 1-4 Barton Street, tel: 01225 420119. This branch of the justly popular chain is next door to the Theatre Royal. **£**

The Sausage Shop, 7 Green Street. For a midday takeaway, try a gourmet sausage in a roll (tomato bread, walnut, etc) from the shop's new takeaway outlet.

Inside the Moon and Sixpence

Shopping

Compact, diverse and with a number of luxury shops not normally found outside London, Bath has the best shopping centre in southwest England. It has done for centuries. Several of Jane Austen's characters are depicted shopping in its lanes. In *Northanger Abbey* Isabella Thorpe, 'saw the prettiest hat you can imagine, in a shop window in Milsom Street', and in *Persuasion* Sir Walter stands in a shop in Bond Street and counts 87 women go by with 'not one tolerable face among them'.

South of the Pump Room

Generally, the higher you climb in Bath, the more exclusive the shops. The area below the Pump Room is dominated by mainstream chain stores (Marks & Spencer, British Home Stores, Littlewoods, Boots). There are, however, notable exceptions, including Rose Marie, on Abbey Green, offering elegant outfits for special occasions.

North of the Pump Room

In Abbey Churchyard you will find several shops aimed primarily at tourists, including the National Trust Shop and a branch of the English Teddy Bear Company. North of Westgate the shops begin to get more interesting, with Union Street leading on to Old Bond Street and then Milsom Street in one long shopping thoroughfare, plus fruitful side streets such as **Northumberland Passage**, **Union Passage** and **Shires Yard** (designer labels, expensive lingerie, Timberland, fine shoes). At the top of Union Street Disney Store, Next, County Casuals) **Upper Borough Walls** harbours Susan Gillis-Browne, a classsy dress shop, and Monsoon. Here Burton Street (with a small branch of Liberty) turns into **New Bond Street** where Laura Ashley and Jigsaw cater to different dress tastes.

Old Bond Street and **Milsom Street** have a roll-call of well-known names, including Jacques Vert, Gap, Gieves & Hawkes, Bally, Waterstone's, Hobb's, Austin Reed, Jaeger, Culpeper and the Savoy Taylors Guild. Also here is the much-loved 19th-century department store Jolly's.

Higher still are high-class purveyors of furnishings, antiques and fine art, many specialising in 18th-century items. For a run-down (including locator map) of the many antique shops in the Upper Town obtain the leaflet 'Bath & Bradford on Avon antique Dealers Association' from the Tourist Information Centre. Even if you are not planning to buy antiques it is worth walking up to **Saville Row** (near the Assembly Rooms) for the wonderful toyshop Tridias and, close by in the Great Western Antique Centre in **Bartlett Street**, Jessie's Button Box selling buttons and clasps from the 18th century to the present day.

*Northumberland Passage
Store on Union Passage*

A famous London offshoot

Get ahead hats in Rose Marie

Walcot Street fleamarket

The Podium

High Street, Broad Street and Walcot Street

This area is worth exploring for offbeat shops. **Broad Street** offers the Italian food specialist Pasta Galore and Rossiters department store. In **Green Street**, leading off from Broad Street, is the Sausage Shop (from Stilton and apple to vegetarian and gluten-free). Leading up to the London Road from High Street, **Walcot Street** is a rich hunting-ground for crafts, antiques, junk and wrought-ironwork. Haliden Oriental Rugs has a large selection of antique items. Further up, Walcot Reclamation specialises in architectural antiques and garden furniture.

On Saturdays, a fleamarket is held in the warehouse next to Walcot car park on Walcot Street. On a different tack, visit the **Podium** (Northgate Street), a modern mall devoted to small speciality shops such as Crabtree & Evelyn and Cawardine's (teas and coffees).

Bridge Street and Pulteney Bridge

Just before the bridge Droopy & Browns offers wildly romantic evening wear. Around the corner on **Grand Parade** (next to the indoor market) is Long Tall Sally, for well-made clothes for tall women. The shops on the **bridge** itself are generally too small to offer anything very interesting, but there is the Bath Stamp and Coin Shop, a good quality florist and Rosalind Mellor selling antique lace, bed linen, wedding veils, etc. Just over the bridge is another London offshoot, the General Trading Company (by appointment to virtually the whole Royal family), selling striking ornaments, rugs and cushions.

Museum Shops

All the museums have a shop. The most interesting is the one attached to the **British Folk Art Collection** (the Vineyards), which is filled with attractive, well-made crafts.

Active Pursuits

Ballooning

One of the most memorable views of Bath is from a balloon. Bath Balloon Flights, 24 Gay Street, tel: 01225 466888, operates all year round. Balloons are launched from Royal Victoria Park and flights last about one hour.

Ballooning over Bath

Boating

On the Avon, the Boating Station, Forester Road (signposted from Sydney Gardens) hires out traditional wooden rowing boats, punts and canoes by the hour or day between April and September (March and October weekends only). Tel: 01225 466407. Organised river trips run to Bathampton Weir and back (1 hour) from below Pulteney Bridge.

The Kennet and Avon Canal Trust operates narrow-boat cruises from Bath Top Lock (tel: 01225 462313). For self-drive cruises through the lovely Limpley Stoke Valley, the Bath & Dundas Canal Co (Brass Knocker Bottom, Monkton Combe, tel: 01225 722292), 5 miles (8km) southeast of Bath (off the A36), has small electrically-powered boats for between four and 10 passengers.

Messing about in boats

Caving

Cheddar Gorge and Showcaves runs caving expeditions for anyone aged 12–60. Full equipment is provided. Tel: 01934 742343.

Fishing

Chew and Blagdon lakes, off the A368 west of Bath, offer good fly fishing for large rainbow and brown trout between March and October. Boats may be hired for the day (book in advance).Though the lakes are popular with very experienced anglers, novices are welcome, with beginners days, casting lessons and tuition weeks available. For more details, contact: Woodford Lodge, Chew Stoke, Bristol BS18 8XH, tel: 01275 332339

Golf

Bath Golf Club, Sham Castle. 18-hole course open to non-members (with handicap certificate) except at weekends; equipment may be hired. Tel: 01225 463834.

Bowood House (*see page 58*) also offers an 18-hole golf course, set in Capability Brown's Bowood Great Park. Open to non-members. Tel: 01249 822228.

Pony trekking

Wellow Trekking Centre, Little Horse Croft Farm, Wellow. A range of rides available for novices and experienced riders, from half-an-hour to a half-day 'pub ride'. Open all year round, except Christmas Day. Tel: 01225 834376.

Getting There

By car

Bath lies within easy reach of both the M4 and M5 motorways, making it easily accessible from London, Wales and the Midlands. However, the lovely countryside around the city can make slower 'A' roads more attractive options, in particular the A4 across the Wiltshire Downs (*see page 55*) and the A46 which winds through the Cotswolds to Stroud and Cheltenham.

By coach

National Express runs a direct coach service between London Victoria bus station and Bath every two hours on the hour during the day and every hour in the evening. The journey takes around 3¼hrs. To book, tel: 0990 808080.

Bath's bus station is opposite the train station, on the south side of town, a short walk from the centre.

By train

Great Western operates a fast InterCity service between London Paddington and Bath Spa (from 1hr 20 minutes) and Bristol Temple Meads (1hr 40 minutes); details from London Paddington, tel: 0171 2626767. Regional Railways South Wales & West runs trains from Cardiff (1hr 10 minutes) at approximately half-hour intervals throughout the day.

Bath Spa Station is to the south of the city centre (an eight-minute walk from the Abbey). It is served by a taxi rank and has a branch of Hertz on the premises.

Bath Spa Station

By air

The nearest airport is Bristol (north of the city, near the junction of the M4 and M5 motorways. Airport information: 01275 474444.

Getting Around

Bath is a compact city best suited to walking. A variety of maps are available from the Tourist Information Centre in Abbey Churchyard. The open-top bus tours which offer an all-day hop on and off service can be a useful way of getting around (*see Facts for Visitor, page 75*).

Car Rental

This is well worth doing if you want to explore the countryside and villages around Bath. Car rental firms include:

Eurodollar, tel: 01225 481898
Budget, tel: 01225 482211
Hertz, tel: 01225 337759/442911

Buses

Though unlikely to be necessary in the city centre, buses can be useful for making short trips to nearby villages, such as Bradford-on-Avon or to visit the American Museum at Claverton Down. For information, contact the bus station, tel: 01225 464446.

Trains

Trains to Bristol Temple Meads (not Bristol Parkway, which is some way from the city centre) leave from Bath Spa Station throughout the day and take between 10 and 25 minutes depending on the type of train. Rail enquiries: 0117 9294255.

The easiest option

Taxis

Taxi ranks are found at Bath Spa station, the Orange Grove, Milsom Street and New Orchard Street.

Bath Spa Station: 01225 425678
Abbey Radio Taxis: 01225 465843
Orange Grove Taxis: 01225 447777
Rainbow Taxis: 01225 460606
Ace Taxis: 01225 427411

Bike hire with a difference

Bike hire

Bikes can be hired from Avon Valley Cyclery, Arch 37, behind Bath Spa Station, tel: 01225 461880/442442. The towpath of the Kennet and Avon canal offers easy, safe cycling and passes through glorious countryside. In Bradford-on-Avon, bikes can be hired from Lock Inn Cottage, 48 Frome Road, tel: 01225 868068.

Car parks

Parking is notoriously difficult in Bath. Park & Ride schemes – Newbridge Road (Monday to Saturday), Bath University (Saturday only), Lansdown playing fields (weekdays only), Odd Down (Monday to Saturday) – try to dissuade visitors from bringing vehicles into the city centre. Parking is free (there is a small charge for the ride) and buses leave at regular 15-minute intervals.

On-street parking is restricted (less so on Sundays) and requires you to buy a parking card from shops displaying the parking card logo (a red C containing a small black P). Illegally parked cars will be swiftly clamped or even removed.

Car parks are found at the following locations: Avon Street, Charlotte Street (below Royal Victoria Park), Walcot Street, the Podium (a multi-storey next to the Hilton Hotel in Walcot Street with a three-hour limit), Ham Gardens (near the bus station), Manvers Street (near South Parade) and Sports Centre and Bath Cricket Club (both near the North Parade).

Facts for the Visitor

*Take the tour bus route
or devise your own*

Tourist Information

The Tourist Information Centre is located in Abbey Churchyard. The staff can help with a wide range of enquiries on both Bath and the surrounding area, and offer a free room booking service. Tel: 01225 462831.

Outside Bath

Bradford on Avon, tel: 01225 865797

Bristol, tel: 01179 260767

Cheddar, tel: 01934 744071

Glastonbury, tel: 01458 832954

Warminster, tel: 01985 218548

Wells, tel: 01749 672552

Cash dispensers and Link machines

Abbey National: Bath Street

Barclays: Stall Street and Manvers Street

Halifax: Southgate and The Corridor

Lloyds: Lower Borough Walls and Milsom Street, Wellsway and Newbridge Road

Midland: Milsom Street, Southgate

National Westminster: High Street, George Street

Nationwide: Old Bond Street

Royal Bank of Scotland: Quiet Street

TSB: Upper Borough Walls

Travel services

American Express, 5 Bridge Street, tel: 01225 444800; foreign exchange 01225 444767.

Sightseeing tours

Open-top bus tours (either Citytour or The Bath Tour) offer a hop on and off ticket valid all day, so can be a useful way of getting from one sight to another.

Guided walks are led by the Mayor's Honorary Guides. They leave from outside the Pump Room in Abbey Churchyard daily (except Saturday between October and April) at 10.30am and 2pm (Sunday 2.30pm) and last around two hours. For details, tel: 01225 477000.

On Friday evenings you can join a 'ghost walk' around some of the many sites in Bath that are believed to be haunted. Tours (charge made) begin from the Garrick's Head, next to the Theatre Royal (tel: 01225 463618).

Opening times

Though most museums and sights in Bath are open year-round, many attactions in the countryside are open only between March and October or have restricted opening times in winter. Even in summer, some places (such as Dyrham Park and the American Museum) are not open in the morning. Before planning a trip, be sure to check the opening times of the sights you want to see (opening hours are given in the routes section of this guide).

Shops offer late-night shopping on Thursday (normally until 6.30pm, but until 8pm in the run-up to Christmas). Some shops open on Sunday.

Postal services

The main post office is in New Bond Street (open Monday to Friday 9am–5.30pm, Saturday 9am–1pm).

Main post office

Emergencies

Help is at hand

Police, ambulance, fire brigade: 999
Bath Police Station, Manvers Street, tel: 01225 444343
Royal United Hospital, Combe Park, tel: 01225 428331

Disabled access

Though a Georgian city centre doesn't lend itself to access for the disabled, Bath City Council does its best to help. For information on access, contact the Access Officer, tel: 01225 477670.

The Shopmobility Centre, 4 Railway Street (Tuesday to Friday 9.30am-4.30pm, Saturday 9am-1pm), hires out manual or powered wheelchairs and electric scooters for nominal cost to anyone with limited mobility. Book in advance, tel: 01225 481744.

Spectator sports
Rugby
Watch top Rugby Union at the Recreation Ground (near Pulteney Bridge), tel: 0891 884554.
Horse racing
Bath races are held at regular intervals between April and September. For fixtures contact the Tourist Information Centre.

Bath For Children

In spite of its sophisticated image, Bath makes an effort to appeal to children as well as adults. On summer weekends the parks hold regular entertainments, while the river and the Kennet and Avon Canal offer an assortment of canal and river trips (*see page 71*). The Roman Baths is sufficiently fun to capture the imagination of older children, and the Postal Museum (*see page 28*) appeals to budding philatelists. Parents with young children should seek out the toyshop Trididas (*see page 69*) and the tiny puppet theatre beneath Pulteney Bridge (*see page 29*).

A family day out

The region around Bath offers a wealth of things to do and see. Within easy striking distance is Bristol Zoo (daily 9am–6pm/5pm in winter, closed Christmas Day; free for under-threes) and Bristol Ice Rink (tel: 0117 929 2148 for session times). Outdoor tastes are catered for in the Mendip Hills, whose limestone is riddled with caves. The most spectacular of these are Wookey Hole, near Wells (*see page 46*), and Cheddar Showcaves (*see page 45*). At Cheddar children (and adults) can follow the Crystal Quest, while older children join a caving expedition.

On the Crystal Quest and inside Longleat Safari Park

One of the top regional attractions is Longleat, whose famous safari park is just one of a whole range of child-oriented attractions (*see page 52*). Also here, set in the delightful Longleat Forest, is one of the highly successful Center Parcs (tel: 01623 411411). On the other side of Bath, near Chippenham, is the Castle Combe Skid Pan & Kart Track, where a club for junior drivers is held on the first Sunday of every month (birthday parties for children aged 10–15 also catered for); tel: 01249 782101. More sedate are the steam railways of the region, including East Somerset Railway at Cranmore (*see page 51*) and the Avon Valley Railway at Bitton (*see page 39*).

All aboard the East Somerset Railway

Accommodation

Booking ahead is essential in Bath, especially in summer and on weekends. If you do arrive in Bath without accommodation, you can save a lot of legwork by using the Tourist Information Centre's free room booking service. Failing this, your best bet is to explore Bathwick (over Pulteney Bridge), the Upper Bristol Road or the Wells Road – areas rich in B&Bs.

Royal Crescent Hotel

City
££££ (over £200 per night double)
The Royal Crescent Hotel, 15–16 The Royal Crescent, tel: 01225 739955. The ultimate address in Bath (no hotel sign is allowed to mar the facade). Antiques, paintings, individually decorated rooms. Secluded garden at the back. Notable restaurant. Central.
Priory Hotel, Weston Road, tel: 01225 331922. Gothic-style 18th-century house west of Royal Victoria Park. Comfortable, individual and quiet.

£££ (over £120 per night double)
The Queensberry Hotel, Russell Street, tel: 01225 447928. Small hotel occupying three Georgian houses knocked together. Comfortable and characterful, though some rooms on the small side. The esteemed Olive Tree restaurant is in the basement.
Bath Spa Hotel, Sydney Road, tel: 01225 424257. Near Sydney Gardens and set in its own extensive grounds. All comforts, including spa. Excellent restaurant.
Francis Hotel, Queen Square, tel: 01225 463411. Another famous address, this time on John Wood the Elder's square.
Somerset House Hotel and Restaurant, 35 Bathwick Hill, tel: 01225 466451. Attractive Georgian house, which is family-run. Noted for its fine food. Dinner is included in the price.

Bath Spa Hotel dining room

££ (over £60 double)
Bloomfield House, 146 Bloomfield Road, tel: 01225 420105. Upmarket B&B in large 19th-century neoclassical house. Some rooms with four-poster or half-tester beds. High up on the south side of Bath, off the Wells Road. Longish walk to the centre. Non-smoking.
Holly Lodge, 8 Upper Oldfield Park, tel: 01225 424042. Large Victorian house on the south side of Bath. Emphasis on service and comfort. Excellent breakfasts. Frilly 'nouveau' furnishings.
Paradise House Hotel, 86–88 Holloway, tel: 01225-317723. Characterful hotel with attractive rooms, good views, and beautiful garden.

Dukes Hotel, Great Pulteney Street, tel: 01225 463512. Comfortable accommodation in Georgian townhouse. Good value for the location.

Sydney Garden Hotel, Sydney Road, tel: 01225 464818. Comfortable and pretty rooms.

Great Pulteney Street

£ (under £60 double)

Holly Villa Guest House, 14 Pulteney Gardens, tel: 01225 310331. Convenient Bathwick location. Attractive and comfortable. Some rooms with en suite. No-smoking.

Meadowland, 36 Bloomfield Park, tel: 01225 311079. No Georgian interiors, but pleasant and comfortable. No-smoking.

The Hollies, Hatfield Road, Bath, tel: 01225 313366. Reasonably priced accommodation (all with private bath or shower rooms) in grade II listed Victorian property.

One of many B&Bs

Outside Bath

££££

Combe Grove Manor Hotel & Country Club, Brassknocker Hill, Monkton Combe, tel: 01225 834644. Luxurious 18th-century house set in landscaped gardens and woodland, 2 miles (3km) from the city centre. Spa and sports facilities, including tennis courts, indoor and outdoor pool. A recommended retreat.

££

Box House Hotel, London Road, Box, tel: 01225 744447. Attractive Georgian hotel 4 miles (6km) from Bath. Set back from the busy London Road.

Old Manor Hotel, Trowbridge Road, Widbrook, Bradford-on-Avon, tel: 01225 777393. 16th-century manor farmhouse. Restaurant.

Bradford Old Windmill, Masons Lane, Bradford on Avon, tel: 01225 866842. Stay in a converted windmill. No-smoking.

£

Brunel's Tunnel House Hotel, High Street, Saltford, tel: 01225 873873. Mid-way between Bath and Bristol. One-time home of Isambard Kingdom Brunel. Rooms individually furnished. En suite facilities.

The Manor House, Monkton Combe, tel: 01225 723128. Attractive 16th-century manor offering very reasonably priced accommodation (private facilities). Breakfast served until noon.

The Old Court House, Corston, tel: 01225 874228. Historic building (1600) 3 miles (5km) from Bath. Cosy and comfortable. 'Hanging' Judge Jeffreys, who tried those involved in Monmouth's rebellion, stayed here in the 1680s. No-smoking.

Index